MARSDEN HARTLEY

GAIL R. SCOTT

MARSDEN HARTLEY

ABBEVILLE PRESS   PUBLISHERS   NEW YORK

FRONT JACKET
Down East, Young Blades, 1940
Oil on panel, 40 × 30 in.
Jon and Barbara Landau

BACK JACKET
Painting No. 1, 1913
See plate 31

FRONTISPIECE
Fig Tree, c. 1924–25
Oil on canvas, 24¼ × 20½ in.
Private collection, Kansas City, Missouri

EDITOR: **Nancy Grubb**
DESIGNER: **Nai Chang**
PRODUCTION MANAGER: **Dana Cole**
PICTURE RESEARCHER: **Lisa Peyton**

Chronology, Exhibitions, Public
Collections, and Selected Bibliography
compiled by Gail R. Scott. Gail Levin,
author of the forthcoming Marsden
Hartley catalogue raisonné, provided
assistance with the list of public
collections.

All marginal quotations are by Marsden
Hartley; for sources, see page 183.

First edition

Library of Congress Cataloging-in-Publication Data

Scott, Gail R.
    Marsden Hartley / Gail R. Scott.
        p.   cm.
    Bibliography: p.
    Includes index.
    ISBN 0-89659-879-9   :
    1. Hartley, Marsden, 1877–1943—
Criticism and interpretation.
I. Title.
ND237.H3435S34   1988   88-10464
759.13—dc 19   CIP

CONTENTS

INTRODUCTION

One afternoon in the 1920s critic Herbert Seligmann was viewing the pictures at Alfred Stieglitz's Intimate Gallery. "A tall figure entered," he later recounted, "culminating in a lean, acquiline, bare, almost Roman head, the face deeply and vertically lined, a man of luxury, it seemed, for he wore a fur-collared overcoat and carried a gold-headed cane. The Ambassador of Poland, perhaps, I thought to myself. It was, in fact, Marsden Hartley—elegant even though he might be starving."[1] Seligmann's anecdote captures the physical aspect of the man and hints at the aura that even today surrounds Hartley's life and art. With his prominent features and piercing blue eyes, Hartley more than once in his writings likened himself to the eagle: solitary, proud, a seer into distant spaces, always, as he noted in his autobiography, "sitting on the edges waiting to be pushed off into the illimitable airs."[2]

Hartley's was a life dedicated to exploring and experimenting, a life spent poised on the edge of the next new adventure, the next new aesthetic horizon. Above all else, he wanted to avoid stagnation and repetition. His solitary and peripatetic life, marked by ceaseless searching, inconsistencies, and uncertainties, is not readily molded into the neatly linear stylistic chronologies favored by art historians. His career, spent moving from style to style, might appear at first glance to be choppy and eclectic. By contrast, the careers of his colleagues Georgia O'Keeffe, Arthur Dove, and John Marin proceeded in more orderly fashion, thereby yielding more readily to historical examination and critical recognition. The unwieldiness of Hartley's life and art accounts to some degree for the fact that his work has received little in-depth analysis until relatively recently.

Since his death in 1943 the significant art historical landmarks have been sparse: a 1944 dual exhibition with Lyonel Feininger at the Museum of Modern Art in New York; the insightful but never fully realized work of Elizabeth McCausland, who championed Hartley's cause in the late 1930s and in 1952 wrote what would be the only monograph on him for over thirty years; and finally, in 1980, a major retrospective exhibition and substantial catalog by Barbara Haskell at the Whitney Museum of American Art.[3] After 1980 the momentum rapidly increased, with published collections of his essays and poetry; several exhibitions on particular themes—Dogtown, Maine, and

1. Milton Avery (1893–1965)
Marsden Hartley, 1943
Oil on canvas, 36 × 28 in.
Museum of Fine Arts, Boston;
The Hayden Collection

2. Marsden Hartley, c. 1940

Nova Scotia; a forthcoming biography by Townsend Ludington; and preparations for a catalogue raisonné by Gail Levin.

Hartley's career is both amplified and complicated by the fact that he was not only a painter but also a published writer who took an active part in some of the most avant-garde literary movements of the early twentieth century. Throughout his life he devoted half of every day to writing, producing an extensive body of essays and poems and carrying on a voluminous correspondence with friends and colleagues. His poetry and essays on art, literature, and the theater appeared, among other places, in the *Little Review, Poetry, Contact,* the *Dial,* the *Seven Arts,* and *American Caravan.* In addition, one volume of essays

(*Adventures in the Arts,* 1921) and three of poetry (*Twenty-five Poems,* 1922; *Androscoggin,* 1940; and *Sea Burial,* 1941) were published during his lifetime. With the exception of a number of catalog statements and an unpublished autobiography, "Somehow a Past," he wrote relatively little about his own art but was an acute commentator on the artists and movements of his day.

At times, Hartley's paintings are upstaged by the man and his legend: his rootlessness; his poverty—largely resulting from lack of sales and critical acceptance; the contradiction between his lonely, shy manner on the one hand and, on the other, his intense affection and regard for certain friends, both male and female; his homosexuality, which contributed to his feelings of alienation from an American society that frowned on such behavior and to his preference for life in Europe, where he found compatible associates. As Peter Plagens once observed, the artist has been "lauded more for his sheer survival" of his suffering than for his art, forcing on him "a false retrospective heroism."[4] This book, then, will concentrate on the paintings, examining them in the context from which they emerged but relegating the legend to the background.

When we focus on Hartley's *paintings,* all else becomes subordinate and his achievement becomes clear. The eclecticism of his early years, his aesthetic wanderings, and the all too apparent frailties of personality give way to what is ultimately important: the quality of the painting, its expressiveness, its impact on viewers today, and on the artists who are his heirs. The influence of Hartley on the generation of artists who followed him is a subject ripe for exploration. Painters as diverse as Milton Avery, Mark Rothko, Philip Guston, Robert Indiana, and Alex Katz found inspiration in the pure painting, the direct presentation, the vocabulary of intense color and mute space that resonate in Hartley's late masterpieces.

Hartley strove all his life to achieve (with varying degrees of success) an art that emerged directly out of felt experience—his own and, by extension, humanity's. More than most of his contemporaries he sought a mental or, at times of greatest inspiration, a spiritual dimension in his painting and poetry. Never satisfied with mere surface appearances, Hartley produced an art that demands probing, and it is the deeper meanings—what Elizabeth McCausland called the "shared universal experiences"[5] of solitude and tempest, personal fragility, and courage in the face of loneliness or death—that most distinguish his contribution to modern American art.

"What I have to express is not handled with words. It must 'come' to the observer. It must carry its influence over the mind of the individual into that region of him which is more than mind. The pictures must reach inward into the deeper experiences of the beholder—and mind you they are in no sense religious tracts—there is no story to them or literature—no morals—they are merely artistic expressions of mystical states—these in themselves being my own personal motives as drawn from either special experiences or aggregate ones."

THE CIRCLE BEGINS

Hartley's claim to the Yankee tradition was geographical as well as spiritual. He was born in 1877 to English immigrant parents living in the mill town of Lewiston, Maine. As the youngest child of nine, whose mother died when he was eight, Hartley spent a lonely childhood. His father, unable to care for the boy, left him for a number of years with an older sister in the neighboring town of Auburn. With nature as his main companion, Hartley acquired a love of flowers—the trillium, dogtooth violet, and Jack-in-the-pulpit—as he roamed the fields and streams of his rural environs. He left school at the age of fifteen and worked in a shoe factory in Auburn for a year until, in 1893, he went to Cleveland, Ohio, to join his father and stepmother, Martha Marsden (whose name he later adopted to replace his given name, Edmund).

There, while working as an office boy in a marble quarry, Hartley began taking art lessons from a local artist, John Semon, and later attended an outdoor painting class with Cullen Yates, a Paris-trained Impressionist. In 1898 Hartley received a scholarship to attend the Cleveland School of Art, and his artistic career began in earnest. One instructor, Nina Waldeck, took special interest in him. Telling him that his face (which he thought homely) bore a striking resemblance to Ralph Waldo Emerson's, she gave him a copy of Emerson's *Essays*.[1] This book, which he carried in his pocket and read continually for the next few years, was, he stated later, "to provide the religious element in my experience."[2] Emerson's philosophy of self-reliance, individualism, and life's open-ended possibilities no doubt struck a deep chord

". . . The virtue of yankee upbringing spiritually speaking is of more downright value to me than any past heritages."

3. *Hall of the Mountain King*, 1908
Oil on canvas, 30 × 30 in.
Private collection

in a young man without family support, lacking even a high school education, and struggling to find direction as a person and an artist. Hartley must have gained confidence from such memorable passages in Emerson's "Circles" as "The life of man is a self-evolving circle which from a ring imperceptibly small rushes on all sides outward to new and larger circles, and that without end." Or, from "The Over-Soul," "Those who are capable of humility, of justice, of love, of aspiration, stand already on a platform that commands the sciences and arts, speech and poetry, action and grace."[3]

According to Emersonian transcendentalism, perception is a process of looking beyond the commonplace fact, beyond the forms of nature to their spiritual essence. The artist is a seer, one who perceives at once the flux and the unity of all things. Nina Waldeck exemplified this kind of deeper perception for Hartley, and as a result of her influence, Emerson's philosophy shaped his budding career and became a touchstone to which he would return time and again as the circles of his own evolving self widened in the coming years.

In 1899 a trustee of the Cleveland School of Art, Anne Walworth, recognized Hartley as a promising young talent and provided him with a five-year annual stipend of $450 to attend art school in New York. In the fall of that year he enrolled in the New York School of Art, known as the Chase School, where his teachers included Luis Mora and Frank Vincent DuMond. Although Hartley received no direct instruction from William Merritt Chase, he faithfully attended the Saturday morning critiques where the elegantly attired Chase waxed eloquent on the privilege of being an artist. Though skeptical of what he called Chase's "fetish" of the brushstroke, Hartley imbibed his love of the physicality of paint and respected him as "a truth teller," in contrast to what he saw as mere technical bravura in the fashionable but "empty" portraits of John Singer Sargent.[4]

Finding the Chase School too costly as well as too superficial, Hartley switched the next fall to the National Academy of Design, where the tuition was a modest ten dollars per year. Among his teachers there during the next four years were Edgar Ward, Jonathan Scott Hartley (no relation), and Francis C. Jones, none of whom appears to have made a significant impact on his development. Of far greater importance was Hartley's return to Maine in the summer of 1900, after an absence of about seven years. He soon found, however, that he had outgrown the small-town mentality. One woman remembered him from this time as "an interesting conversationalist but so intense that he was almost bewildering."[5] Already he faced the dilemma that would shadow his career: a love of Maine's natural beauty and solitude but an aversion to its cultural backwardness.

Nature proved a better instructor than art school. Hartley spent most of that summer in the countryside, as in his boyhood, making

To miss Florence Dingley

Edmund Marsden Hartley

DEC. 21 - 1906.

4. *Monarch Butterfly*, 1906
Colored pencil on paper,
8 × 6½ in.
Judith and Wilbur L. Ross

delicate small sketches of flowers and butterflies (plate 4). (The next winter, and for many years after, he would spend hours studying the butterfly and rock collections at New York's Museum of Natural History, valuing it as highly as any art museum.) Late in the summer he met Charles Fox and Curtis Perry, who taught art in Portland and ran a summer art commune in western Maine on quasi-socialist principles. Their philosophy accorded with Hartley's high-minded aspirations for art. The aim of the school, he wrote, was "to live the higher life and apply it to their art" and to "study Nature scientifically and ar-

5. *Walt Whitman's House*, 1905
Oil on board, 9½ × 5½ in.
Private collection

tistically."[6] Reinforced by these associations and eager to join the commune the following summer, Hartley was meanwhile gaining confidence that he was pursuing the right course by studying nature as closely as possible. Frustrated that his painting was so gray, he strove to key his colors up to the autumnal brilliance he saw in the surrounding hills. In late October he executed what he called "notes of color," disclaiming them even as sketches since they "disregarded accuracy of drawing and modelling wholly for the sake of . . . color."[7] These "notes of color" have not survived, nor have any paintings as yet been definitively dated to before 1905.

In fact, little is known about Hartley's life from 1900 to 1905. His letters to a friend, Richard Tweedy, reveal that for a time he considered going into the Episcopal ministry and that his religious fervency and his love for nature and art were closely allied. After 1900 he continued to return to Maine every summer for eleven years, living in cheap rented quarters or abandoned shacks in the Stoneham Valley near Center or North Lovell. It was "raw living"—terribly isolated, with cold nights and a long walk to get supplies—but he found the views of the White Mountains worth the hardship. Details of this existence are scanty, but it is clear that Maine played an important role in the early development of Hartley's artistic vision.

In 1904, his stipend from Walworth at an end, Hartley was forced to take a job as an extra with a New York theater company, and it was during this period that he became immersed in the second literary influence on his art and thought, the poetry of Walt Whitman. He was probably already familiar with Whitman's poetry when, on a 1905 tour with the theater company in Philadelphia, he made a pilgrimage to Camden, New Jersey, to paint Whitman's house at 328 Mickle Street (plate 5). Radiating a modest warmth, like the poet to whom it pays tribute, this is a tiny jewel of a painting.

Around this same time Hartley met Horace Traubel, editor of the socialist newspaper the *Conservator*. Traubel had been a longtime aide and literary adviser to Whitman in his later years, and after the poet's death devoted much time and effort to perpetuating the Whitmanesque poetic tradition. Traubel's editorials in the *Conservator* called for art that stemmed directly from life and urged the creation of poetry and pictures that visibly affected the reader or viewer and throbbed with all the energy of life itself.

Whitman's poetry, springing as it did from felt experience rather than any literary tradition, American or European, was the first-generation response to Emerson's call for American poets, artists, and scholars to create a new national voice. Hartley, part of a second generation of artists answering this call, wanted an art that offered more than pretty pictures skillfully painted. Despite his provincial beginnings, his indifferent art training, and his almost total lack of formal

14

secondary education, Hartley had found, by an uncanny intuitive sense, two of the most brilliant luminaries of late nineteenth-century America, and he claimed them as his intellectual and spiritual guides.

Hartley continued the Whitman connection even after he left the theater company and went back to Maine in the fall of 1906. Traubel was involved in a network of Whitman enthusiasts in Boston, New York, and Philadelphia who held occasional "Whitman dinners" and informal gatherings of poetry reading, discussion, and camaraderie, which Hartley occasionally attended. Among these Whitman devotees was the Portland, Maine, publisher Thomas Bird Mosher, who befriended Hartley in 1905 and corresponded with him. Hartley's association with these men (which he later wrote about in an unpublished essay, "Peter Doyle and the Whitman Group") formed an important bond of male comradeship for the young artist-poet living in almost total seclusion in the remote hills of Maine. He wrote ardent, affectionate letters to Traubel—love letters in tone and feeling—timidly showing him the poems he had begun to write (his earliest dated poem is 1904), describing his painting, and confiding both the ideals and the uncertainties of his evolving career.

Through Mosher and Traubel, Hartley found work during the summer of 1907 at Green Acre, a retreat in Eliot, Maine, where the Congress of Religions convened to discuss universal brotherhood and such religious and mystical subjects as the unification of Eastern and Western spiritual traditions. This exposure to Eastern religions no doubt had considerable impact on Hartley's thought. His letters from that summer, while making little mention of specific topics discussed, do speak rapturously of the fellowship and communion he found with certain friends there and gratefully acknowledge their support of his art. Mrs. Ole Bull, wife of the famed violinist, gave Hartley his first one-man exhibition in her home adjacent to the Green Acre complex, and he considered the $90 in sales a promising mark of success.

Hartley remained in Eliot through the fall of 1907 and then moved to Boston for the winter, presumably living on his earnings from the summer. From 1906 to 1909 Hartley's unique style of Impressionism gradually began to take shape. He later attributed this development to the influence of Giovanni Segantini (1858–1899), a lesser-known Swiss painter whose work he first encountered in the European art journal *Jugend*. Segantini, who lived an isolated existence high in the Alps, had developed a kind of self-styled Impressionism consisting of small, elongated dabs of pure color known as the "Segantini stitch." Hartley admired Segantini because living so close to his mountains he knew their topography intimately and could render their character with authenticity. Hartley claimed that by emulating Segantini's technique he was able to heighten his color and portray *his* mountains with greater intensity.

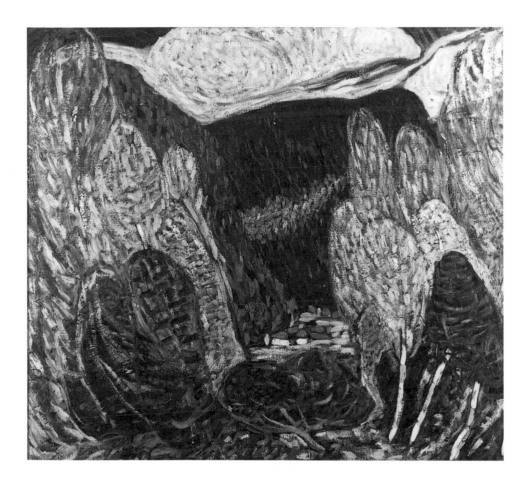

OPPOSITE
6. *Storm Clouds, Maine*, 1906–7
Oil on canvas, 30½ × 25½ in.
Walker Art Center, Minneapolis;
Gift of T. B. Walker Foundation,
Hudson Walker Collection, 1954

ABOVE, LEFT
7. *Landscape No. 36*, c. 1908–9
Oil on canvas, 30⅛ × 34 in.
University Art Museum, University
of Minnesota, Minneapolis;
Bequest of Hudson Walker from
the Ione and Hudson Walker
Collection

ABOVE, RIGHT
8. *Landscape No. 16*, 1908
Oil on academy board,
11⅞ × 8⅞ in.
Private collection

In *Storm Clouds, Maine* (plate 6) Hartley's newly adopted approach is readily apparent. Dominated by gray clouds looming over the dark mountainside, the picture is nonetheless luminous. Streaks of bright autumn color zigzag across the deep purple and brown of the evergreens. Another motif borrowed from Segantini can be seen in the solid cloud formations, which Hartley would use to great effect in later landscapes. The high vantage point of the scene pulls the viewer inescapably into the drama of the storm as it courses overhead.

Compositionally, the paintings from this early body of work are astonishingly original. *Landscape No. 36* (plate 7) presents an unusual vista telescoped through two clumps of trees down to a cluster of small buildings at the foot of a mountain. There is no precedent, at least among the American Impressionists, for such a format. Maurice Prendergast, John Twachtman, George Inness, and Edward Lawson all favored garden scenes, rolling meadows, and a soft tonal palette. Hartley's forms, including the brooding clouds, seem to lean inward with physical and metaphorical weight, creating a landscape of the mind as much as of nature. In *Landscape No. 16* (plate 8) the artist narrowed his focus to a group of birch trees, creating a rhythmic pattern from their crisscrossed trunks. Inscribed on the back is a poem that begins "October Lies—Dying / The dead dance frantically!" alluding to the ghostly swaying of the birch trees in the wild October winds. The theme of dying autumn would echo through Hartley's painting and verse for the rest of his life.

Describing his preference for late autumn with its deep purples and greens and sedate cream and gray tones, Hartley told Traubel, "It is like a strong resonant octave of Chopin, out of Grieg."[8] Indeed, the title for a 1908 painting, *Hall of the Mountain King* (plate 3), must have been inspired by the last movement of *Peer Gynt,* Edvard Grieg's incidental music set to Henrik Ibsen's play. This title and several others from the same period indicate Hartley's burgeoning literary and mystical inclinations. In *Cosmos* (plate 9), a title probably deriving from Whitman's frequent use of the word, Hartley attempted to portray the spirit behind the landscape forms. He informed Traubel that he was "happily contented to be climbing the heights and the clouds by the brush method . . . rendering the God-spirit in the mountains." More-

9. *Cosmos,* 1908–9
Oil on canvas, 30 × 30⅛ in.
Columbus Museum of Art,
Columbus, Ohio; Gift of
Ferdinand Howald

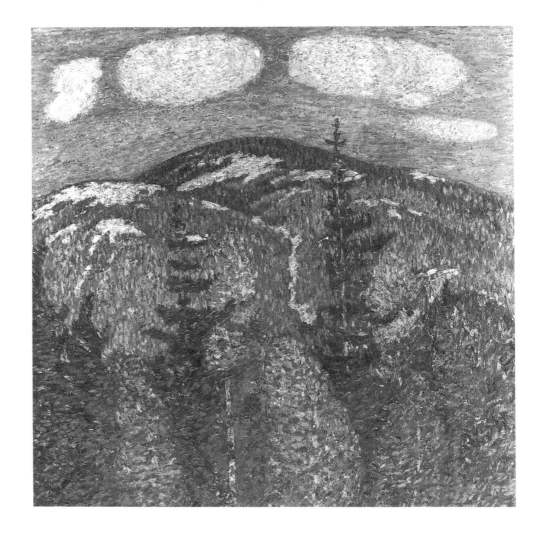

over, he was pleased that woodsmen who knew these mountains "by daily intercourse with them" praised and appreciated his work.[9] To capture both the everyday appearance and the "God-spirit" of the landscape was Hartley's two-edged purpose.

To render the subtle tonal variations beneath the overall whiteness of winter was another challenge that Hartley took up during this period, in a series of landscapes called Songs of Winter (plate 10). The hills are saturated with pale mauve, pink, and blue; patches of white snow highlight the trees and mountain crevices; and the shadows, in true Impressionist fashion, are purple and blue. The gray tones Hartley worried over have evaporated.

The winter of 1908–9, which brought ferocious weather and continual blizzards, Hartley spent alone in a cabin in North Lovell. In

10. *Landscape (#3—Song of Winter)*, c. 1908
Oil on board, 9 × 12 in.
Private collection

19

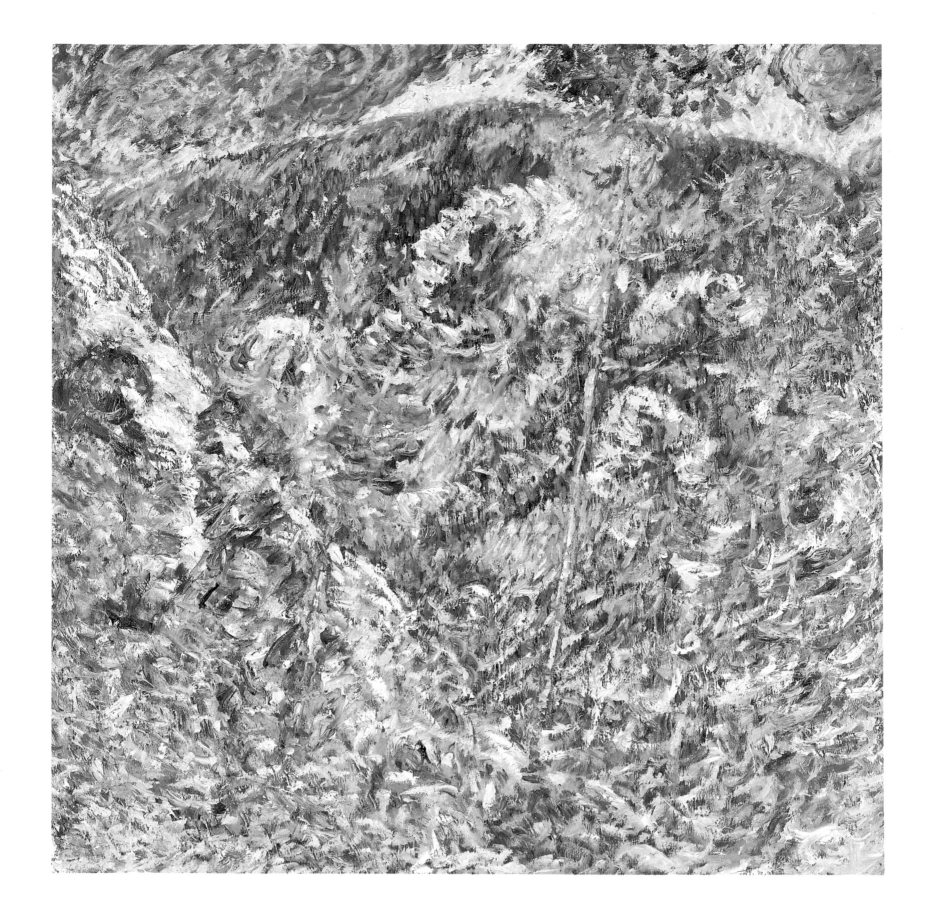

Winter Chaos, Blizzard (plate 11), the weather itself dictated a looser stroke and freer motion than the tightly controlled and regimented brushstroke of *Storm Clouds*. Shapes are barely discernible in the swirl of paint. Hartley had taken a giant leap from the gentle atmospheric snow scenes of such American Impressionist predecessors as Lawson and Twachtman. With no one else for company he turned to self-portraits, producing a series of wild-eyed drawings of himself executed with the same agitated stroke as the paintings (plate 12). Together the paintings and drawings powerfully communicate the "winter chaos" the artist endured.

Hartley was pleased with the work of 1906–9—satisfied with his newly liberated color and with his newly mastered ability to rapidly seize the most striking characteristics of a subject. In 1908 he had exhibited a few canvases at the Rowlands Gallery in Boston and subsequently sold a painting to Desmond Fitzgerald, a prominent Boston collector of Impressionist paintings. In the spring of 1909 Hartley took his paintings to Boston again to show them to Maurice and Charles Prendergast, who were impressed with the bold intensity of the work. They wrote letters of introduction for him to William Glackens, a member of the New York group of painters known as The Eight.

In the ten years since he had left Cleveland, and the five since leaving art school, the circles of Hartley's experience had rushed outward on all sides. With the Prendergasts' letters in hand, he confidently set off again toward New York, this time with a body of strikingly original paintings that suggested fresh drafts of cold Maine air.

OPPOSITE

11. *Winter Chaos, Blizzard*, 1909
Oil on canvas, 34 × 34 in.
Philadelphia Museum of Art;
Alfred Stieglitz Collection

12. *Self-Portrait*, 1908
Crayon on paper, 12 × 9 in.
National Museum of American Art, Smithsonian Institution, Washington, D.C.; Museum Purchase

"My work embodies little visions of the great intangible. . . . Some will say he's gone mad—others will look and say he's looked in at the lattices of Heaven and come back with the madness of splendor on him."

2

NEW AND LARGER CIRCLES: 291 AND EUROPE

The year 1908, just prior to Hartley's return to New York City, was a watershed year in American art, a year in which the dominating force on the American art scene, the National Academy of Design, finally began to weaken. Neither as entrenched nor as dogmatically authoritarian as the older European academies, the National Academy nevertheless dictated the prevailing taste in portraiture and pleasantly painted Barbizon-style landscapes. Though it counted among its members the three innovators of the nineteenth century—Albert Pinkham Ryder, Winslow Homer, and Thomas Eakins—they were singular, controversial figures, with very few disciples and no significant public following.

In 1908 the Academy refused to exhibit the work of George Luks, one of the energetic young painters of urban low life in the circle of Robert Henri. In support of Luks, Henri, John Sloan, William Glackens, and a few others withdrew their works, showing instead at the National Arts Club. They became known as The Eight, a group that would help propel American art from provincial academicism toward

13. *Painting No. 48, 1913*
Oil on canvas, 47³⁄₁₆ × 47³⁄₁₆ in.
The Brooklyn Museum, New York;
The Dick S. Ramsay Fund

"... the same feeling [on first viewing a work by Albert Pinkham Ryder] *came over me in the given degree as came out of the Emerson's Essays when they were first given to me—I felt as if I had read a page of the Bible in both cases. All my essential Yankee qualities were brought forth out of this picture and if I needed to be stamped an American this was the first picture that had done this—for it had in it everything that I knew and had experienced about my own New England—even though I had never lived by the sea—it had in it the stupendous solemnity of a Blake picture and it had a sense of realism besides that bore such a force of nature itself as to leave me breathless."*

Valley views from earlier work, but now inhabited by dying, broken trees, barren rocks, and the same massive clouds he had first borrowed from Segantini and now found even more solidified by moonlight in Ryder. These are among Hartley's most expressive, anguished works. In his typically piquant style, Paul Rosenfeld later summarized them as "powerful and memorable expressions of the starvation of a generation, the suffering and abandonment by the world which every sensitive spirit in the states feels for long stretches of time."[1]

It has recently been pointed out that Ryder was far more in tune with his time than his reclusive nature would indicate and that his paintings are in fact allegorical statements of the isolation and dislocation of the era.[2] Hartley had never painted simply picturesque scenery, but seeing Ryder's visionary work lent credibility to his belief in landscape as a pictorial battlefield portraying inner conflict. Hartley's Dark Mountain paintings are contemporary counterparts of a Wagnerian realm of gloom and foreboding. Thus the results of Hartley's introduction to 291 set the course for his career along two points of his artistic compass: European modernism, with its breakthrough discoveries in form and color; and America—most specifically the Yankee tradition of Hartley's roots, reinforced by the visionary and transcendental view of nature expressed by Emerson, Whitman, and now Ryder.

That the Dark Mountain landscapes reflected the artist's despondent mood was corroborated by Alfred Stieglitz, who later claimed that Hartley had been on the verge of suicide.[3] Perhaps the elation of his New York debut was overshadowed by the disappointment of making no sales to alleviate his always precarious financial state. Learning of his plight, Montross offered him a small stipend of four dollars per week (the amount Hartley said he required to live and work in Maine) for two years. Montross wanted no paintings in exchange for the stipend, and his gift, though meager, enabled Hartley to continue working. Between November 1909 and the spring of 1912 he painted in North Lovell, traveling down to New York periodically to pursue his "education" among the various artists and photographers at 291.

For virtually the rest of his life this would be the pattern: retreating to some isolated location for his painting and writing but drawn irresistibly back to New York (or Paris, or Munich) for the stimulus of the art milieu. Writing in 1910 of the dilemma posed by these two poles of his existence, he said: "It is the incongruous thing in my entire life, this isolation. . . . My work requires it—but I myself have no need or use for it—Perhaps once on a time I found isolation imperative—I think all chrysalides do—all embryos go for the underside of the leaf in the time of body-changes—preparing for the final reassertion-resurrection—the establishment of the entity. But now I've come up

to the outside of my casements."[4] *Landscape No. 20, Resurrection* (plate 17), painted at this same juncture, could be seen as symbolizing emergence. Though related to the Dark Mountain landscapes, it is warmer in tone, less angular and threatening in form. The central figure, surrounded by a womblike aura, resembles a chrysalis shedding its cocoon. Hartley's world was opening up for him, and he was increasingly eager to move out into the crowd.

Over the next four years he would confront nearly every form of European modernism, his own painting often directly reflecting his most recent encounter. Much the same was true for the other young Americans in the Stieglitz circle—Dove, Marin, Maurer, Walkowitz, and Weber—who went abroad in the first decade of the century. In assessing the impact of Post-Impressionism on these artists, it is all too easy to dismiss their work as derivative of the seemingly more advanced Europeans. In 1910 the educational vacuum created by the overthrow of the tradition-steeped academies left the field wide open, and for the first time came the awareness that art is built from two

16. *Desertion*, 1910
Oil on wood panel, 14 × 22 in.
Private collection

17. *Landscape No. 20, Resurrection,*
    1909
    Oil on academy board,
    13½ × 11½ in.
    Private collection

primary sources: individual experience and other art. This was the exhilarating freedom that greeted these young artists when they stepped off the boat in Europe. With the conviction that intuition, personal vision, and experience guided them, the Americans (Hartley included) absorbed and appropriated the new discoveries of modernism—spontaneity in color, direct expression, flat, simplified forms, and the breakdown of traditional spatial relationships—with ingenuous candor and with surprisingly little apology for "being influenced." The spirit of the time (much as in New York during the 1950s, with the rise of Abstract Expressionism) seemed to allow for especially fluid crosscurrents of thought and discovery.

Matisse was the first of the European giants Hartley encountered at a 291 exhibition, in the spring of 1910. The most radical aspect of

Matisse's work—color—was totally absent from this particular selection, which comprised only drawings and black-and-white photographs of such important paintings as *Joie de vivre* (1905–6) and *The Blue Nude* (1907).[5] Nonetheless, the work generated much excited discussion by Max Weber and others in the 291 set who had seen the originals and knew Matisse.

Although Hartley had no apparent firsthand knowledge of Matisse's color, his palette did undergo significant change at this time. The pastel hues of earlier Impressionist works such as *Maine Landscape* from 1908 (plate 18) gave way in *Still Life No. 12* (plate 19) to

18. *Maine Landscape,* 1908
    Oil on panel, 11½ × 9 in.
    Martin and Enid Packard, Comstock Park, Michigan

19. *Still Life No. 12,* 1910
Oil on canvas, 20 × 16 in.
Walker Art Center, Minneapolis;
Gift of Berta H. Walker, 1971

20. *Red Tree,* 1910
Oil on cardboard, 14 × 11 in.
National Museum of American
Art, Smithsonian Institution, Wash-
ington, D.C.; Gift of Flora E. H.
Shawan from the Ferdinand
Howald Collection

a predominance of primary colors, applied in thick, rich strokes of paint. The white cloth (more white than Hartley had ever used) with blue shadows in the folds accentuates the purity of the color and thrusts the still-life objects forward on the picture plane.

In *Red Tree* (plate 20), the handling is even freer, recalling Matisse's loose, wide brushstroke. *Red Tree* is an intriguing combination of Fauvist color and compositional elements from Hartley's earlier works such as *Landscape No. 36,* where a central passage opens into deep, slightly enigmatic space. He wrote to his niece that he was working "almost wholly from the imagination . . . using the mountains only as backgrounds for ideas."[6] The new stylistic discoveries, however exciting, remained incidental to his continuing concern with the problem of landscape as idea, the Emersonian notion that all things in nature correspond to a state of mind, which it is the artist's work to translate

RIGHT

21. *Waterfall,* 1910
    Oil on academy board, 12 × 12 in.
    University Art Museum, University
    of Minnesota, Minneapolis;
    Bequest of Hudson Walker from
    the Ione and Hudson Walker
    Collection

BELOW

22. Pablo Picasso (1881–1973)
    Landscape. La Rue des Bois, 1908
    Oil on canvas, 39⅝ × 32 in.
    Collection, The Museum of
    Modern Art, New York; Gift of
    David Rockefeller

OPPOSITE

23. *Landscape No. 32,* 1911
    Watercolor on paper,
    14¹⁄₁₆ × 10¹⁄₁₆ in.
    University Art Museum, University
    of Minnesota, Minneapolis;
    Bequest of Hudson Walker from
    the Ione and Hudson Walker
    Collection

into paint. In *Waterfall,* from 1910 (plate 21), the brushstrokes of pure color nearly overpower form altogether. The rapidly executed jabs of paint, giving only a suggestion of rocks, falling water, and trees, correspond in this Emersonian sense to the turgid flow of the spring freshet. The wide swaths of paint now replace the tightly structured "stitch" borrowed from Segantini.

In the spring of 1911 Hartley saw the 291 exhibition of eighty-three drawings and watercolors by Picasso, including both Rose Period Harlequin works and more recent examples of Analytical Cubism. Shortly thereafter Hartley painted *Landscape No. 32* (plate 23), which closely resembles Picasso's 1908 proto-Cubist landscapes. Although not all the works from that show have been identified, *Landscape. La Rue des Bois* (plate 22) serves as a useful comparison to Hartley's effort. The two works are compositionally similar, consisting of a building seen amidst a labyrinthine pattern of crossed bare tree trunks. Hartley likewise adopted the long, hatched brushstroke of thinly applied paint. The differences are even more telling. Picasso's

On Walt Whitman and Paul Cézanne: *"They are the gateway for our modern esthetic development, the prophets of the new time. They are most of all, the primitives of the way they have begun, they have voiced most of all the imperative need of essential personalism, of direct expression of direct experience."*

24. *Still Life No. 11*, 1911
Oil on canvas, 9½ × 7½ in. University Art Museum, University of Minnesota, Minneapolis; Bequest of Hudson Walker from the Ione and Hudson Walker Collection

aim was to simplify and compress the landscape elements of trees, building, and sky into a tightly organized pictorial statement. Hartley's purpose was primarily emotive rather than pictorial. He used the Cubist devices of intersecting planes and spatial ambiguity to create a relentless tension on the tiny house, lost in the tangle of trunks. Subjecting the now familiar theme of the deserted farm to Cubist formal language, he discovered a new way to express the psychic condition of isolation and desolation. The idea has not changed, only the means of conveying it.

The year 1911 marked Hartley's first serious investigation of Cézanne, though at first, as in the case of Matisse's work, only through black-and-white illustrations.[7] That summer he executed a number of small still lifes of two pears on a plate, studied at close range with intense concentration and portrayed with a limited color range of rich browns, golds, and blacks (plate 24). Though inspired by Cézanne, *Still Life No. 11* is unmistakeably Hartley's in composition. Set against a dark triangle formed by the sharply angled drapery and tabletop, the pears, with their soft, voluptuous curves, sit Buddha-like in the center of this hieratic arrangement.

After he finally saw Cézanne paintings in the flesh when Arthur B. Davies arranged for him to visit the Havemeyer collection in New York that winter, Hartley's still-life arrangements became more ambitious. Over the years Cézanne would mean many things to him, but even at this early date he intuitively grasped the essence of Cézanne's contribution: his genius for selection and penetration, and his ability to present objects simply and directly while expressing what Hartley called the "palpitancy" beneath the surface. As he told Stieglitz, Cézanne showed him "how personal one can become through striving to express the impersonal." These little studies of pears embodied Hartley's effort to achieve this "essential personalism," or authentic individual expression, by attempting to convey the living quality beneath the surface.[8]

Later that spring, with help from Davies and Stieglitz in arranging financial assistance, Hartley found himself sailing for Europe, and by mid-April 1912 he was in the heart of the Parisian art world. Paris in 1912 offered an extraordinary confluence of art and ideas, and in the short space of two weeks Hartley sampled a large portion of it, visiting the Louvre and Luxembourg museums, the Salon des Indépendants, the Salon des Beaux-Arts, Notre Dame, Sainte-Chapelle, and the Panthéon, as well as all the major galleries, where he saw work by Vincent van Gogh, Paul Signac, Paul Gauguin, Georges Seurat, Picasso, Braque, Matisse, and Cézanne. Hartley was able to sublet the studio of Lee Simonson, a painter-friend he had known in North Lovell, and there he began to paint again, at first pursuing the kind of still-life studies he had been doing prior to his departure. *Still Life No. 1*

(plate 25) vibrates with a Matisse-like weaving of colorful patterns and shapes. The little black chest with its decorative inlay plays off against the gold-patterned black drapery on the left, while the same effect occurs between the cloth on the right and the red, orange, and green fruit. The bowl of fruit tilts precariously to one side, offsetting the more regular perspective of the chest.

Soon after his arrival in Paris, Hartley became acquainted with a small German coterie that gathered at the Restaurant Thomas and included a young sculptor, Arnold Rönnebeck, and his cousin, Karl von Freyburg. Hartley felt an immediate affinity for his new German friends, with whom he felt he had more in common than the more frivolous, billiard-playing Americans. It was also with this group that Hartley found the homosexual subculture that would later make Germany so appealing to him. Simultaneously, he discovered the work of Wassily Kandinsky and Franz Marc through their new almanac, the *Blue Rider (Der Blaue Reiter),* published earlier that year in Munich as well as Kandinsky's revolutionary little book, *On the Spiritual in Art,* both of which he enthusiastically recommended to Stieglitz. Since one of the *Blue Rider*'s primary aims was to link the art of past ages and diverse ethnic groups with the present as a way of revealing the universal substance beneath all forms of expression, the almanac contained fascinating illustrations of art from many cultures. Hartley's comprehension of German was still meager, but it is conceivable that his German friends translated passages of the impassioned text for him.

The prevailing interest in African and Polynesian sculpture spurred Hartley to visit the Musée d'Ethnographie du Trocadéro in Paris to see its vast collections of ethnographic art from all over the world, which he began to incorporate in his compositions. *Still Life No. 1* includes a piece of Pueblo pottery, a small Zia jar with a geometric design, while *Indian Pottery (Jar and Idol)* (plate 26) depicts an Acoma pot with a bird image and a carved wooden figure resembling Kwakiutl sculpture.[9] More subdued in color and texture than the still lifes done earlier that summer, this latter work features brick red and sandstone hues and dry, scumbled texture that are appropriate to the subject. "One can no longer remain the same," Hartley wrote to Stieglitz, "in the presence of these mighty children who get so close to the universal idea in their mud-baking." But the artist also recognized that to imitate the art of primitive people merely for intellectual or formal purposes was inauthentic; his art must result, he added (echoing Kandinsky's famous phrase), from "spiritual necessity" and "revolts of the soul."[10]

Soon after his arrival Hartley, like so many others, found his way to the famous Saturday evenings of Gertrude and Leo Stein, frequented by Picasso, Matisse, Robert and Sonia Delaunay, and an

25. *Still Life No. 1,* 1912
Oil on canvas, 31½ × 25⅝ in. Columbus Museum of Art, Columbus, Ohio; Gift of Ferdinand Howald

26. *Indian Pottery (Jar and Idol)*, 1912
Oil on canvas, 20¼ × 20¼ in.
Private collection, Dallas

assortment of visiting Americans. Because of his own literary inclinations, he and Gertrude had long conversations about writing and discovered a common interest in William James, who had been her mentor at Harvard.[11] Hartley borrowed her copy of James's *Varieties of Religious Experience* (1902) and read extensively in it that summer.

Having sat for portraits by Picasso and Matisse, Stein had in turn done word portraits of those two painters, which Stieglitz published in *Camera Work*.[12] From this notion of literary and pictorial portraits, and from his reading of *Varieties of Religious Experience*, Hartley conceived of his own unique type of portrait—the portrait of a word. *Raptus* (plate 28) refers to a passage in James's chapter on mysticism in which he describes the state of *raptus* or *ravishment* experienced by Christian mystics such as Saint Theresa and Saint John of the Cross— a state of ecstasy beyond intellect which imagery or verbal description fails to convey.[13] Adapting the Cubist convention of incorporating incidental words into the composition, Hartley's painting focuses on the word itself. Lying on a white recessed plane below concentric circles, the letters are intersected by one of the converging rays, symbolizing the mystical union achieved in the state of *raptus*.

Raptus was intended to be the first in a series, and although Hartley did no others quite like it, *One Portrait of One Woman* (plate 27), probably executed in 1916 after his return to New York, belongs to the same genre. It is his version of Gertrude Stein, in response to her abstract portrayal of him in a curious play titled *IIIIIIIIII*. Rendered in brilliant red, white, and blue (the colors of both the French and American flags, from the two countries Stein loved), the painting is a symbolic evocation. Using a centrally located word, *moi*, and a teacup (Hartley often had tea at the Stein's) against a hierarchy of arches, it conveys Stein's impressive personality in both abstract and concrete terms.[14] The title, reflecting that of Stein's play, shows Hartley's playful appreciation of her literary style, manifest especially in the word portraits, where constant repetition of *one* as a substitute for *I* intensifies the tension between objectivity and intimacy.

Stirred by James's treatise on mystical experiences, Hartley found inspiration that fall from reading Jakob Boehme, Meister Eckhart, Johannes Tauler, Heinrich Suso, and Jan van Ruysbroeck. His affinity for the German sensibility—encountered through his circle of German friends and by reading the German mystics and the ideas in the *Blue Rider* and *On the Spiritual in Art*—quickened his interest in spiritual concerns, especially in contrast to French art, which he felt was superficial and lacking "inward sturdiness" or soul.[15]

In *Abstraction* (plate 29), Hartley continued his effort to portray the ineffable in purely nonrepresentational terms without even a word (as in *Raptus*) as reference point. Around the same time he experimented with another way of translating nonvisual experience into vi-

ABOVE
27. *One Portrait of One Woman,*
c. 1916
Oil on composition board,
32 × 21⅜ in.
University Art Museum, University of Minnesota, Minneapolis; Bequest of Hudson Walker from the Ione and Hudson Walker Collection

PAGE 40
28. *Raptus,* 1913
Oil on canvas, 39⅜ × 31¾ in.
The Currier Gallery of Art, Manchester, New Hampshire; Gift of Paul and Hazel Strand in memory of Elizabeth McCausland

PAGE 41
29. *Abstraction,* c. 1912–13
Oil on canvas, 47 × 39½ in.
Private collection

sual imagery when he embarked on a series of musical equivalents stimulated by preludes by Johann Sebastian Bach, César Franck, and other composers. He was already familiar with the notion of musical associations in painting from his own earlier work and from discussions of the subject in the Stieglitz circle. Both the *Blue Rider* and *On the Spiritual in Art* devoted much attention to the notion of a synthesis of music and painting as another manifestation of the structural relatedness of different art forms. In addition, Hartley had visited the studio of Robert Delaunay and had possibly also seen the work of František Kupka. But in a typically defensive mode he claimed to be the only one attempting this kind of expression and dismissed Delaunay's work as too theoretical, "like a demonstration for chemistry or the technical relations of color and sound."[16]

Musical Theme (Oriental Symphony) (plate 30) translates the flow and texture of music in thinly painted color washes inspired by Cézanne's watercolors, which Hartley had admired at the Steins. Hieroglyphic markings suggest musical staffs, clefs, and obscure notations, which he later claimed were in the vein of "automatic writing."[17] Included in these works are signs with mystical import, such as eight-pointed stars and three intersecting circles, as well as the seated Buddha figure and the three hands lifted in the Indian sign *abhaya mudra* (have no fear), which give the "Oriental" aspect to this particular canvas.

In November 1912 Hartley traveled to London, taking with him several still-life paintings done earlier that summer, which he hoped to exhibit at the Chenil Gallery with the help of the sculptor Jacob Epstein (whom he had met at the Steins') and the painter Augustus John. Hartley visited the British Museum, where he was overwhelmed by the African, Egyptian, and Assyrian art but dismissed the Elgin Marbles as being too sweet. He also saw paintings by Kandinsky and was convinced that his own new work, which he called "subliminal or cosmic cubism," was different from the Russian's, being the result not of aesthetics or theories but "of spiritual illuminations."[18] This series of Intuitive Abstractions, including the Musical Theme paintings, relies heavily on the compositional matrix of Analytical Cubism, with receding planes that bleed together and are at once opaque and transparent. Hartley's admiration for Picasso is clear. Perhaps, following Gertrude Stein's lead, he perceived a difference between Picasso and the French artists, who Hartley claimed were interested only in the refinement of sensation. Picasso, on the other hand, had "a depth of understanding and insight into the inwardness of things," and he was "doing very exceptional things of a most abstract psychic nature. . . ."[19]

Hartley identified with what he interpreted as Picasso's greater inner perception, yet the distinctions between their work reveal that

". . . By getting as close to the true idea of religion, of spirituality as it is possible for us to get . . . we would be in possession of the only tangible relationship to the deity in things."

the real source of Hartley's creative vision at this time lay in the same vein he had been tapping all along. While Picasso's genius penetrated "the inwardness of things," it nevertheless took *things*—the objects of a still life, a figure, a landscape—as a starting point. Hartley, on the other hand, relied on the conviction that the reality of things rested in their transcendental relation to the divine.

Eager to visit Germany and meet the Blue Rider artists, Hartley arranged a three-week trip to Berlin in January 1913, where he found warm hospitality from Arnold Rönnebeck and his family. On his return to Paris he stopped in Munich and was deeply impressed by an exhibition of Franz Marc's paintings at the Galerie Thannhauser. Hartley met with Kandinsky at his home and, with Rönnebeck acting as translator, described his own work and discussed their mutual interests. He hoped to exhibit his Intuitive Abstractions in Munich at the Galerie Goltz, and after returning to Paris sent several of them there for review. In an exchange of letters with Marc, Hartley elicited an invitation to show with the Blue Rider group at the autumn salon in Munich, the Herbstsalon. His German connection was growing stronger by the week.

In May, when Lee Simonson reclaimed his studio, Hartley packed up for a more permanent residence in Germany. Before his departure Gertrude Stein visited his studio twice, where she saw, among others, *Painting No. 1* (plate 31). In a letter to Stieglitz she stated her impression of Hartley's work, distinguishing his originality from that of Kandinsky, Picasso, Delaunay, and Matisse. "He has used color to express a picture," she said, "and he has done it so completely that while there is nothing mystic or strange about his production it is generally transcendent."[20] While the resemblance of *Painting No. 1* to Kandinsky's Improvisations is undeniable, Hartley took great pains to stress to Stieglitz and others the American sources of his work, claiming "I could never be french—I could never become german—I shall always remain American—the essence which is in me is American mysticism just as Davies declared it when he saw those first landscapes."[21]

Hartley arrived in Berlin on May 17, 1913, in the midst of the festivities surrounding the marriage of the kaiser's daughter, one of several massive spectacles celebrating what the kaiser declared to be a Hohenzollern year. The pageantry accompanying these events included military parades and torchlight processions, complete with banners, martial music, and cheering crowds. Beneath the euphoria, however, was the geopolitical tension that was about to detonate in the Great War.[22] The revolutionary position of the Blue Rider artists comes into clear focus against the backdrop of this apocalyptic fervor in prewar Germany. In stark contrast to the kaiser's glorification of Prussian military strength, Kandinsky and Marc in the afterword to their almanac proclaimed the time as "the epoch of great spiritual-

31. *Painting No. 1,* 1913
   Oil on canvas, 39¾ × 31⅞ in.
   Sheldon Memorial Art Gallery,
   University of Nebraska, Lincoln;
   F. M. Hall Collection

32. *The Warriors,* 1913
Oil on canvas, 47¾ × 47½ in.
The Regis Collection, Minneapolis

OPPOSITE
33. *Forms Abstracted,* 1913
Oil on canvas with painted frame,
39½ × 31¾ in.
Whitney Museum of American Art,
New York; Gift of Mr. and Mrs.
Hudson Walker and exchange

ity."[23] These artists and their colleagues were the Nehemiahs of the twentieth century, prophesying that the breakdown of scientific materialism would result in the very dissolution of matter, ushering in a new spiritual order.

With his growing appreciation of all things German, Hartley was glad to be out of Paris, which he found too "bohemian," lacking "mental order," and "fearfully over-ridden with art cults." Paris had helped to free him intellectually and spiritually, he told Stieglitz, but in Berlin he felt he had discovered his "essential self."[24] Fundamentally apolitical, he could respond with equal enthusiasm to both the prewar pageantry and the artists' hopes for a new social order.

These two converging forces found expression in a series of abstractions done over the next two years. Reflecting the time and place, such works as *Painting No. 48* (plate 13), *The Warriors* (plate 32), *Forms Abstracted* (plate 33), and *The Aero* (plate 34) celebrated both the old and new in the style of the future. *The Warriors*—the most topical in subject matter—figuratively portrays the military proces-

34. *The Aero,* c. 1914
Oil on canvas with painted frame,
42 × 34½ in.
National Gallery of Art, Washington, D.C.; Andrew W. Mellon Fund

sional for the marriage of Princess Victoria Louise: the entrance through the Brandenburger Thor of the kaiser's special guard of cuirassiers, dressed in white uniforms and riding white horses. Thin washes of paint with the white ground showing through suggest shimmering sunlight. The four principal officers on blue, red, and white horses form a hierarchical arrangement (by now a familiar part of Hartley's formal vocabulary) before red and gold cloudlike aureoles. The equestrian troops, seen from the rear, are, as he later described it, "soldiers riding into the sun—a fact to take place not so long after—for all of these went out into the sun and never came back."[25]

Painting No. 48, a more abstract image, similar in composition and texture to the earlier *Abstraction,* is suffused with a mystical aura, stemming in part from the glowing color, in part from the symbolic association of signs: the cross and eight-pointed star, the numeral *6* (signifying the six days of creation), and the mandorla with the figure *8* (signifying Christ's resurrection, which occurred on the eighth day after his entry into Jerusalem). The correlation between Hartley's state of mind and the theme of resurrection in *Landscape No. 20, Resurrection* (plate 17) from 1909 surfaces again in these Berlin abstractions, possibly because, as Gail Levin observed, Hartley was experiencing a kind of psychological and aesthetic rebirth in Germany.[26]

The blue and red horses in *The Warriors* naturally bring to mind the work of Franz Marc, whom Hartley finally met in May 1913. The borrowed motif is even more obvious in *Forms Abstracted,* where the reclining white horse resembles Marc's *White Bull.* Hartley's partitioning of the composition probably derives from Bavarian glass painting (*hinterglasmalerei*), a folk art that caused much excitement among the Blue Rider artists, all of whom collected numerous examples of it (as did Hartley). In his typical fashion, Hartley adapted the simplicity of style and even certain motifs for his own purposes while appreciating the glass paintings as unique expressions of religious symbolism.[27] Radiating from the horse and circling the painted frame of *Forms Abstracted* are variations of the simple eight-pointed star, which he claimed to see everywhere in Germany and which he adopted for its life-giving implications.[28] Like many of his contemporaries, Hartley was fascinated with the new technology of air flight, which in Germany focused on the dirigible airship being developed as part of a war armament project sponsored by the kaiser himself. *The Aero* attempts to convey the "extase d'aéroplane" or "soul state" of an airplane, symbolized by the red fireball of its engines and the aerial view of flags and banners signaling its flight.[29]

In November, Hartley sailed for America, taking with him the Intuitive Abstractions and his first Berlin paintings for his third one-man exhibition at 291, which took place in January 1914. A statement accompanying the works was the artist's first published piece of writing, a manifesto of artistic individualism. Echoes of the *Blue Rider* can be heard in the intense, rhapsodic tone as well as in the theme: disclaiming the old forms and proclaiming Cézanne, Henri Rousseau, Odilon Redon, and the American Indian as prophets of a new artistic age.[30] After only five months in America, Hartley returned to Germany at the end of April, immersing himself with renewed enthusiasm in the Berlin art world. Sharing the prevailing fascination with primitive art, as he had in Paris, he visited Berlin's Museum für Völkerkunde, which had very large collections of ethnographic art, including American Indian displays. As if to reaffirm his Americanness, he planned a series of paintings with an Indian leitmotif, which he called his "Amerika" pictures. Iconographic studies of *Indian Fantasy* (plate 35) have

"Art creates itself out of the spirit substance in all things. . . . A picture is but a given space where things of moment which happen to the painter occur. The essential of a real picture is that the things which occur in it occur to him in his peculiarly personal fashion. . . . The idea of modernity is but a new attachment to things universal—a fresh relationship to the courses of the sun and to the living swing of the earth—a new fire of affection for the living essence present everywhere."

49

shown that the bird image, canoes, and other symbols and designs derive from both Pueblo and Plains Indian sources.[31]

The *Amerika* series and other pictures such as *Pyramid and Cross* (plate 36; probably painted somewhat later) utilize one of the dominant features of Indian design, seen in everything from beadwork to weavings—symmetry. Ideally suited to Hartley's preference for formal, triangular-based formats, symmetry became an important part of his compositional vocabulary. A variation was the compartmentalized canvas, which in *Berlin Ante-War* (plate 37) underscores the two forces at work in the German zeitgeist. The Prussian equestrian soldier parades in a cloud of glory against a circle containing a white horse with the numeral *8* on his haunch. In the lower partitions (like the

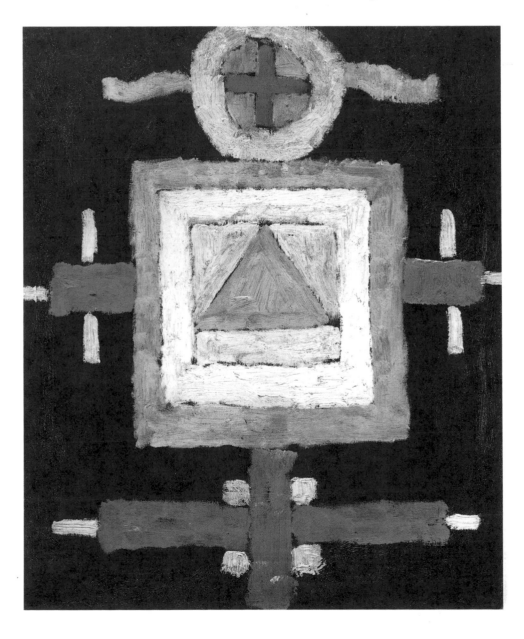

OPPOSITE

35. *Indian Fantasy,* 1914
    Oil on canvas, 47 × 39½ in.
    North Carolina Museum of Art,
    Raleigh

36. *Pyramid and Cross,* 1914
    Oil on canvas, 18 × 15 in.
    Elizabeth B. Blake

predella of an altarpiece) are more bucolic scenes. Encapsulated in this work is the calm before the storm that burst over Europe.

Despite the outbreak of war in August, Hartley remained in Berlin, continuing to paint and ignoring the concern of his friends in Paris and New York. In October he learned that Karl von Freyburg (Rönnebeck's cousin who had become Hartley's intimate friend in Berlin) had been killed in one of the first major battles of the war. With von Freyburg's death came the painful awareness of what the war would mean. This was the first of a number of deaths that would generate some of Hartley's greatest painting and poetry. In the effort to alleviate his own grief, he turned naturally to his art for a means of expression.

The idea for the German Officer paintings had been germinating in the months preceding the war, as Hartley's friends put on their impressive uniforms and went off with their regiments. But in *Portrait of a German Officer* (plate 38), with its black background of mourning, there is the poignant sting of death. Years later, Hartley wrote that von Freyburg "stood as a symbol for all that is inspiring in young life."[32] Several of the paintings in this series (among which *Portrait of a German Officer,* one of the largest canvases he ever painted, is the masterpiece) are personal tributes to von Freyburg, as signified by the various emblems and letters: his initials *KvF, E* for his regiment (the Bavarian Eisenbahn), the regimental patches, banners, and the Iron Cross he was awarded.[33] But like *Raptus,* these paintings are in a larger sense portraits of an idea: of comradeship and youth lost through heroic death. Though later attacked by patriotic American critics for what was perceived as their pro-German sentiment, they are in fact universal in implication, paeans to dead soldiers of whatever nationality.

The German Officer series continued the abstract-portrait idea begun earlier. The paintings in the series have also been compared stylistically to Cubism, utilizing the compositional method of placing flat, faceted forms against a black or neutral background. But unlike the Cubists' structural interpretation of form, Hartley's paintings start from an ideational premise (an elegy to youth and heroism), as numerous critics have observed.[34] Semiabstract emblems were his idiom in 1915, but his later paintings on the theme of death, even though in a realistic mode, are not so very different. *Black Duck No. 1* (plate 140), for instance, is an elegiac portrait of a dead bird and presented in much the same manner—a heraldic image against a dark field. Hartley absorbed the syntax of Cubism not primarily to advance an aesthetic idea but to convey the meaning that evolved from the events and relationships he experienced, an approach that characterized his whole European venture. As he continued working on the series through 1915, his treatment of the subject became less formal, and the centrality of the images gave way to an allover patterning. In *Berlin*

37. *Berlin Ante-War,* 1914
Oil on canvas with painted wood frame, 41¾ × 34½ in.
Columbus Museum of Art, Columbus, Ohio; Gift of Ferdinand Howald

38. *Portrait of a German Officer*, 1914
    Oil on canvas, 68¼ × 41⅜ in.
    The Metropolitan Museum of Art,
    New York; The Alfred Stieglitz
    Collection, 1949

39. *Berlin Abstraction*, 1914
    Oil on canvas, 32 × 26 in.
    The Corcoran Gallery of Art,
    Washington, D.C.; Museum Pur-
    chase, Gallery Fund, 1967

Abstraction (plate 39), the design itself takes over, extending to the border of the canvas; the black background disappears altogether.

In October 1915 Hartley had a critically acclaimed exhibition in Berlin of forty-five of his Paris and Berlin pictures, as well as two groups of drawings, a show that constituted the most significant recognition of his work to date and his only major European exhibition. The reception awaiting both the artist and his German paintings in New York would be less heartwarming.

THE SEARCH FOR CLARITY

Hartley returned to New York in December 1915 after three years in Europe, during which his art had undergone radical changes and his intellectual and aesthetic awareness had expanded enormously. His paintings were to be exhibited at 291 in February 1916, but because they were delayed in transit by the war, the show was postponed until April. The impact of European modernism on Hartley and his colleagues was apparent in the Forum Exhibition of Modern American Painters, held that spring at the Anderson Galleries. Unlike the massive and unwieldy Armory Show three years before, the Forum Exhibition was small in scale (fourteen artists) and presented what the organizing committee intended as a consolidated view of modern art in America. The catalog included statements by the artists and voiced nearly unanimous insistence on an art of personal sensibility, with inner feeling prevailing over intellect. In his remarks Hartley addressed the issue of influence by claiming that "characteristics are readily imitable; substances never," and citing the struggle of Cézanne and El Greco to achieve "their peculiar individual esthetic" (though, he noted with admiration, Cézanne's work showed no trace of struggle).[1] Hartley knew only too well the distance *he* had traveled from Maine to Paris and Berlin.

Since its inception the 291 circle had propounded an ethos inspired in part by Henri Bergson's notion that art evolved from the artist's intuitive response to his subject and to his ever-changing relationship to nature and to other art forms.[2] Poet William Carlos Williams, who mixed with the 291 crowd, recalled that in this period "there had been a break somewhere, we were streaming through, each

"Every painter must traverse for himself that distance from Paris to Aix or from Venice to Toledo. Expression is for one knowing its own pivot. Every expressor relates solely to himself—that is the concern of the individualist."

40. *Purple Mountains, Vence,* 1925–26
Oil on canvas, 25⅜ × 32 in.
Phoenix Art Museum; Gift of Mr. and Mrs. Orme Lewis

thinking his own thoughts, driving his own designs towards his self's objectives. . . ."[3]

When Hartley's Berlin pictures were finally shown at 291 in April 1916, it was to a New York audience prejudiced by anti-German war sentiment. Caught in the wrong place at the wrong time, the paintings suffered the irony of being some of the most original but least appreciated work by an American Post-Impressionist. Unlike his previous fervent catalog statements, the one accompanying these paintings was a brief paragraph aimed at forestalling an interpretation of the works as pro-German or prowar. The images, he claimed, were only those "observed casually from day to day" with "no hidden symbolism"— a remark that then and ever since has caused more controversy than the paintings themselves, which even in 1916 were at least recognized for their impressive power and innovativeness. Prodded by Hartley's denial of hidden symbolism, critics have delighted in disproving his statement by decoding symbolic meanings and tracing iconographical sources.

When critic Charles Caffin commented that "the motive of these is scarcely what has been seen unless it be in the mind's eye,"[4] he was unwittingly pointing to precisely that aspect of the creative process in which Hartley had the most faith: the dictates of the imagination. As Charles Eldredge stated it, "For Hartley the goal was not an occult cryptogram, but a suggestion of the spiritual perceived through the self."[5] The images that mystified his audience *had* been seen "in the mind's eye," in the sense that they were pictorial transformations of people and events that had deeply affected him, and it is precisely this experiential aesthetic, deriving from Emerson and from William James's Pragmatism, that distinguished Hartley from his European colleagues. He relied on James's empirical approach to the subject: namely, that personal inner experience and religious transformation, rather than abstract philosophical notions, were the only authentic form of mystical experience. Painting for Hartley had to be the result of inner revelation, not predetermined by theories of symbolic equivalents of colors and forms.

Coming "home" to America from Berlin, where he had found friends, acceptance, and encouragement, Hartley must have suffered painful alienation in the wake of negative reaction to his German work and the general atmosphere of war-related emotionalism. Mabel Dodge, wealthy art patroness and supporter of numerous social and political causes, purchased *Raptus* and befriended Hartley that winter, though even she found his solipsistic moods difficult. At Dodge's salon, held in her Greenwich Village apartment, Hartley attempted to integrate himself back into the New York scene among such political luminaries as Max Eastman, Hutchins Hapgood, John Reed, and the many artists and poets who gathered there. No doubt the Dodge salon brought to mind similar evenings at 27 rue de Fleurus, for it was at this juncture that Hartley painted his abstract portrait of Gertrude Stein (plate 27). In this and in a number of Cubist-inspired still lifes—such as *Handsome Drinks* (plate 41), with its cocktails, absinthe glass, teacup, and word fragments—Hartley found a more palatable yet no less sophisticated genre.

The same crowd around Mabel Dodge moved to Provincetown, Massachusetts, for the summer (Hartley went along as John Reed's guest), and it was there that the seeds for the future Provincetown Players were sown with the production of plays including Eugene O'Neill's *Moon of the Caribees*. It was a congenial time, with everyone getting into the act by sewing costumes, constructing and painting sets, and acting or directing.[6] While Hartley enjoyed the company of

41. *Handsome Drinks*, 1916
   Oil on composition board,
   24 × 20 in.
   The Brooklyn Museum, New York;
   Gift of Mr. and Mrs. Milton
   Lowenthal

42. *Movement No. 5, Provincetown Houses,* c. 1916
Oil on composition board,
20 × 16 in.
The Metropolitan Museum of Art, New York; The Alfred Stieglitz Collection, 1949

OPPOSITE

43. *Trixie,* 1916
Oil on board, 24 × 20 in.
Private collection

Charles Demuth, Carl Sprinchorn, and William and Marguerite Zorach, he confided his continuing sense of estrangement to Stieglitz, "I lie in bed & hear the sea & the seabirds cry their cry for me & we are not alien."[7] He captured the mood of Provincetown—the ocean, its shifting dunes and long beaches—in a series of abstractions of houses and sailboats. *Movement No. 5, Provincetown Houses* (plate 42) recreates in vivid light-dark contrasts the lively activity of the resort town. Other canvases, including *Trixie* (plate 43), feature a boat's name: a fixed and recognizable sign in a semiabstract field similar in composition to *Handsome Drinks, One Portrait of One Woman,* and the German Officer series.

44. *Sail Boat*, c. 1916
Oil on pasteboard,
15⅝ × 11½ in. (sight)
Columbus Museum of Art,
Columbus, Ohio; Gift of
Ferdinand Howald

OPPOSITE
45. *Compote with Fruit*, 1916
Oil on board, 25 × 20 in.
Mr. and Mrs. Arnold C. Kirkeby,
Rancho Santa Fe, California

Hartley and Demuth remained in Provincetown through the fall
and then sailed for Bermuda, where accommodations were cheap due
to war blockades. Hartley's palette softened under the influence of the
tropical ambience of Hamilton, with its pink and chocolate-brown
houses and its blue-green waters. In works such as *Sail Boat* (plate
44), where sails billow in a full wind against a limpid sky, can be seen
the soothing effect of his Caribbean retreat. These are cool paintings,
delicate and refined, probably done under the spell of Demuth's work.
A far cry from the passionate intensity that fired the Berlin paintings,

46. *Atlantic Window*, 1917
Oil on board, 32 × 25¾ in.
Harvey and Françoise Rambach

OPPOSITE
47. *Three Flowers in a Vase*, 1917
Tempera and tinfoil on glass,
13⅝ × 7⅝ in.
Richard York Gallery, New York

they exemplify the abrupt stylistic shift necessitated by his return to an America that did not accept or understand his work. But with the resilience born of Yankee ingenuity, Hartley was able to start afresh, as if his vision had been washed clean by saltwater and stinging air. By spring, however, he had reached a saturation point with pretty ocean settings. He wrote to Sprinchorn that nature "wearies the eye with so much of its commonness." Nature "just for itself was not enough,"[8] by which he meant, in the Emersonian sense, that the artist must see nature with the creative perception that transforms it from the commonness of just so many picturesque details.

Hartley turned to still life, using the same subdued coloring and dry, almost sand-textured surface, in compositions of detached but elegant formality. *Compote with Fruit* (plate 45) adds a new motif to the still life: a view through an open window—a format he had undoubtedly seen in work by Matisse and André Derain and which would become one of his favorite compositional devices. In *Atlantic Window* (plate 46), he refined this alliance of landscape and still life with a complex interaction of recessed planes and color harmonies. The yellow ocher of the nearby curtain and window frame reappears in the distant hills and in other highlights, while the sweep of the beach, rendered in blues and grays like the vase, further unites foreground and background. Hartley was gradually enriching his newfound restrained vocabulary.

He spent the summer of 1917 at a summer art colony in Ogunquit, Maine, established by Hamilton Easter Field, a wealthy painter and collector. Field and others in the group such as sculptor Robert Laurent were avidly collecting examples of American folk painting on glass and mirrors.[9] Hartley, already familiar with the Bavarian folk tradition, decided to experiment with the technique. Unlike the *hinterglasmalerei*, which dealt with religious subjects, the American versions were most often simple decorative motifs of flowers or fruits, painted on black backgrounds and often using crumpled painted foil to build the images. *Three Flowers in a Vase* (plate 47) depicts a group of fanciful, jewellike flowers rendered in a deliberately naive manner against a brilliant blue ground. The neutral subject matter suited Hartley's current frame of mind, and though the method was taxing, the results were intriguing.

America's entrance into World War I brought many changes to the art community. Among the casualties was 291, which Stieglitz was forced to close in 1917. He did not, however, abandon his artists, and he worked behind the scenes to assist Hartley in finding a dealer who could show his work. Charles Daniel gave him an exhibition in 1918 and a small stipend, which offered the opportunity for travel again. The Southwest attracted Hartley (as it did many of his contemporaries) as a promising setting for work and an inexpensive place to live.[10]

48. *Pitcher and Dipper*, c. 1918–21
Oil on fiberboard, 23⅜ × 18¼ in.
Hirshhorn Museum and Sculpture
Garden, Smithsonian Institution,
Washington, D.C.; Gift of Joseph
H. Hirshhorn, 1966

OPPOSITE
49. *El Santo*, 1918
Oil on canvas, 36 × 32 in.
Museum of Fine Arts, Museum of
New Mexico, Santa Fe

His earlier interest in native American art had been motivated in part by witnessing the excitement it aroused in Europe; by 1918 the American art community was suddenly becoming aware of this rich heritage. Mabel Dodge, having attached herself to the idea of American nativeness, had moved to Taos, bought property, and encouraged Hartley and others to join her. He arrived there in June 1918, eager for the change of scene.

When Hartley painted *Indian Fantasy* in Berlin, his sources were museum artifacts. When confronted with the real thing in New Mexico, he found, unlike his predecessors Robert Henri, George Bellows, and others, that he could not simply adopt Indian subjects as freely as before. *Pitcher and Dipper* (plate 48) depicts two pieces of Indian pottery in traditional still-life manner, fundamentally differing from the earlier abstractions in which he had composed fragments of Indian designs into freely contrived conceptual arrangements. The blue-gray pottery with its black geometric patterning sits on an oblique surface tilted against a richly textured background dominated by blue, gray, and yellow ocher. There is a directness and simplicity in this work that pays tribute to its subject and at the same time shows a delicacy of handling stemming from the artist's work done in Provincetown and Bermuda.

Unlike Mabel Dodge, with her infatuation with the Indian mystique, and unlike the artists who used Indian subjects to paint another form of Americana, Hartley grew during his months in New Mexico to understand this native phenomenon at a deeper level, and in his writings was one of the first to champion it.[11] He appreciated Indian culture for many of the same reasons he had loved Germany in the prewar period—for the pageantry and splendor of its rituals. He attended nearly all the tribal dances in Taos and Santa Fe, but unlike John Sloan or Jan Matulka, he did not depict the dances in his painting. One, however, was the subject of a long poem, "The Festival of the Corn" (published in *Poetry* in 1920),[12] which reflects Hartley's fascination with the intermingling of ancient Indian ceremonies and Catholic liturgical rituals.

Mabel Dodge had already amassed a collection of Mexican *retablos* and *bultos*—carved and painted wooden votive panels—one of which Hartley used as the focal point for *El Santo* (plate 49), a still life that underscores this cultural medley in a subtle way.[13] The *retablo*, depicting Christ carrying the cross, has an austere religiosity and symmetrical format that are intentionally played against the more decorative aspects of the composition: the angled table, the *olla* pot containing a spiky plant, and the striped Indian blanket. Rather than exploiting a native idiom not authentically his own, the artist has utilized its underlying elements: the naïveté, the limited tonal harmonies, the curvilinear rhythms. The still lifes he produced in New Mexico

50. *Arroyo Hondo, Valdez*, 1918
Pastel on cardboard,
17¼ × 27⅝ in.
University Art Museum, University
of Minnesota, Minneapolis;
Bequest of Hudson Walker from
the Ione and Hudson Walker
Collection

"*My work has the abstraction underneath it all now & that is what I was
working toward & what I deliberately set out to do down here, for this
is the perfect realistic abstraction in
landscape.*"

demonstrate Hartley's masterful adaptation of his European sources
to an unmistakably American theme.

His first overtures with the southwestern landscape were in pastels, a medium Hartley favored over watercolor or oil for in situ
sketches because of its chromatic intensity and portability. Daily he
walked great distances into the arroyos around Taos and Santa Fe,
making rigorous, close studies of the topography and the light effects.
He was amazed at the clarity of detail made possible even at vast distances by the brilliant light, which he captured along with the intense
heat of the dry hills in such works as *Arroyo Hondo, Valdez* (plate
50). *New Mexico* (plate 51) depicts a more dramatic desert site where,
as he described to Stieglitz, "great isolated altar like forms . . . stand
alone on a great mesa with immensities of blue around them and that
strange Indian red earth making almost unearthly foregrounds." [14]

Hartley remained in the Southwest (including a brief visit to California) for about eighteen months, during which the course of his art
shifted permanently to landscape and still life—a shift that has generally been interpreted as a retreat from European-based abstraction
back into realism. [15] Hartley, however, justified his position in terms of
a new and much-needed objectivity and clarity. The full import of his
experience is most evident in the paintings of New Mexico he did *after*
he left the region. In *Landscape No. 3, Cash Entry Mines, New Mexico* (plate 52), executed back on the East Coast, the descriptive element is subordinated to a highly charged evocation of nature's
magnificent pulsating rhythms, recalling previous masterpieces such as
Cosmos (plate 9). *Cash Entry Mines* combines many of the same compositional elements first encountered in the earlier paintings: arched

51. *New Mexico,* 1919
    Oil on canvas, 20 × 34 in.
    Portland Museum of Art, Portland,
    Maine; Hamilton Easter Field Art
    Foundation Collection, Gift of the
    Barn Gallery Associates, Inc.,
    Ogunquit, Maine, 1979

52. *Landscape No. 3, Cash Entry
    Mines, New Mexico,* 1920
    Oil on canvas, 27¾ × 35¾ in.
    The Art Institute of Chicago; The
    Alfred Stieglitz Collection, 1949

53. *Landscape No. 5*, 1922–23
Oil on canvas, 23 × 35½ in.
National Gallery of Art, Washington, D.C.; Alfred Stieglitz
Collection

mountain ridges (similar to the hierarchical arrangement in *The Warriors*, plate 32); solid (though now angular) cloud formations; and tiny buildings dwarfed by the mountain. But Hartley's confrontation with abstraction has paid off. Beneath the surface of *Cash Entry Mines* is a new understanding of the dynamics of form and space and of color handling that makes the hills, valley, and sky throb with inner life.

The final phase of Hartley's New Mexico paintings emerged in Berlin, where he returned in 1921. Unable to sustain the intensity of his New Mexico experience and yearning for the friends and cosmopolitan lifestyle of the Continent, he arranged, with the help of Stieglitz and Mitchell Kennerly, for an auction of 117 of his unsold paintings at the Anderson Galleries in May 1921 to raise money for another trip to Europe. When Hartley finally arrived in Berlin he was aware of the changes the war had wrought in art. Perhaps in an effort to strengthen his own position, he had defiantly declared in 1918 that since "the fetish of Paris . . . has been destroyed by the war," the logical step beyond Cubism and Futurism would be new forms of realism. "The return to nature," he predicted, "will show a greater audacity in consulting the rhythms of nature as they exist." [16]

In Berlin, after working on still lifes in oil and lithograph, he embarked in 1923 on a series of Recollections of New Mexico. These paintings, executed five thousand miles away from the Southwest and three or four years after he'd left it, were so audacious that they remained neglected or disparaged until a Neo-Expressionist perspective has recently yielded reevaluation of them. Totally different from the pastel landscapes done on site through careful observation of nature, *Landscape No. 5* (plate 53), *Landscape and Mountains* (plate 54), and *New Mexico Recollections No. 12* (plate 55) are remembered visions

54. *Landscape and Mountains,*
    1922–23
    Oil on canvas, 25¾ × 31¾ in.
    Hirshhorn Museum and Sculpture
    Garden, Smithsonian Institution,
    Washington, D.C.; Gift of Joseph
    H. Hirshhorn, 1966

55. *New Mexico Recollections No. 12,*
    1922–23
    Oil on canvas, 29¼ × 39¾ in.
    Archer M. Huntington Art Gallery,
    The University of Texas at Austin;
    Lent by James and Mari Michener

56. *Cemetery, New Mexico,* c. 1924
Oil on canvas, 31⅝ × 39¼ in.
The Metropolitan Museum of Art,
New York; The Alfred Stieglitz
Collection, 1949

of nature, halfway between landscapes of the mind and powerful evocations of place.

Hartley's term for them—*recollections*—brings to mind Wordsworth's famous definition of poetry (which the literary Hartley might well have known) as "emotion recollected in tranquility." But the artist's sense of irony reversed the romantic notion of tranquility, since these recollections evolved from and partially reflected the turmoil of postwar Berlin, with its social and sexual decadence.[17] Like the earlier Dark Mountain landscapes, the New Mexico Recollections are at once specific and imaginative. These pictures have an unreal quality, yet, as one critic has observed, one sees while driving across the Southwest "landforms that instantly trigger images of Hartley's paintings."[18] Filled with barren hills, turbulent skies, skeletal shapes, gravestones (as in *Cemetery, New Mexico,* plate 56), and twisted, bulbous trees and shrubs, these paintings speak for an entire generation of dislocated American expatriates who longed for contact with their native country yet found there no real nourishment or acceptance. The anguish of these works approaches what Charles Eldredge calls "a twentieth-century Sublime."[19]

The ten-year period that Hartley spent in Europe from 1921 to 1930 is usually considered a "lost decade," and the work issuing from it often dismissed as eclectic, unrealized, and unfocused. The judgment persists even now that these works are somehow un-American and that Hartley, having lived too long abroad, did not devote himself sufficiently to American subjects. While as a whole the paintings and drawings from this period may not equal the innovativeness of the earlier German work or the masterful sweep of the late Maine landscapes and still lifes, this middle period has yet to be fairly examined.

Even Alfred Stieglitz urged his wandering protégé to come home, although he had originally supported Hartley's tenure abroad. But Stieglitz confronted certain economic realities when he opened the Intimate Galleries in 1925, and he found it increasingly difficult to sell Hartley's European paintings. Stieglitz (in company with Paul Rosenfeld and Waldo Frank, his main supporters among the art critics) preached the cult of nationalism (albeit through the medium of semiabstract modernism) almost as vociferously as the more conservative camp of realist and Regionalist artists and critics.[20]

Another factor that has tended to obfuscate Hartley's achievement during these years was his ability to work in radically different modes either simultaneously or in rapid succession. In 1923, while working on still life and the dramatic New Mexico Recollections, he was also engaged with a subject he had not touched since 1909—the figure. In Berlin he found some muscular male boxers and hefty female models who became subjects for a series of pastel drawings (plate 57) in sanguine, outlined in black against a suffused background. These

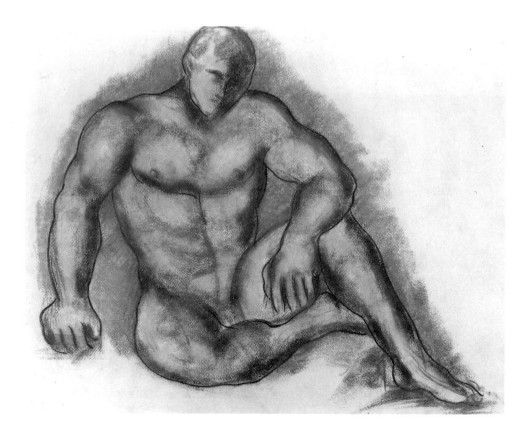

57. *Boxer*, 1923
Pastel on paper, 17 × 22½ in.
Private collection

58. *Still Life with Fruit,* 1924
Oil on canvas, 13 × 21¾ in.
Private collection, New York

On Piero della Francesca's frescoes at Arezzo: *"Perfect union of intellect and the inner vision which for want of a better name is called 'soul.'"*

are classically rendered nude studies, so far on the opposite end of the spectrum from the eerie landscapes that they appear to be by a different hand. But as prototypes for the figures he would do later in Maine, they are definitely Hartley's.

In the fall of 1923 Hartley started out on a long-desired trip through Italy. After a stop in Vienna he settled for eight weeks in Florence, where he studied the Renaissance masters in depth, especially (as indicated in the essays written during his sojourn[21]) Fra Angelico, Masaccio, Michelangelo, and, at Arezzo, the frescoes of Piero della Francesca. His experience with these masters—particularly the monumental simplicity and "humanity" of their figures—made a deep impression on him, providing inspiration for years to come. Hartley spent Christmas in Rome, which he found somewhat exhausting; the simple grandeur of the Coliseum appealed to him more than the extravagance of St. Peter's, especially after the intimacy of Florence. Shortly thereafter he sailed home from Naples. Back in America he again made financial arrangements to enable him to continue working in Europe, this time with the backing of a "syndicate" of five busi-

nessmen, who agreed to pay him an annual stipend of two thousand dollars for four years in exchange for ten paintings a year. By the summer of 1924 he was back in Paris.

Hartley shared the studio of sculptor George Biddle, where he took up work again on the New Mexico Recollection paintings (there are twenty-five of them), as well as a number of luminous still lifes (plates 58 and 59). *Three Blue Fish with Lemons and Limes* belongs to a group he called "Chez Pruniers," after the elegant display windows of the Prunier fish market in Paris, which he loved to study. In this painting, which is reminiscent of William Merritt Chase in both subject and bravura treatment, Hartley seems to delight in the texture of paint itself. The brushstroke is fluid and the approach direct, with a sensuous flair evident in the two-dimensional patterning (note how the curve of the lemons nestles into the sinuous line of the fish bodies).

Having told Stieglitz he wanted to get back to "the French purity of feeling,"[22] in August 1925 Hartley moved to Vence, where, like so many other artists, he could pursue this purity in the light of southern France. Most painters are attracted to the picturesque sea towns on

59. *Three Blue Fish with Lemons and Limes,* 1924
Oil on canvas, 10¾ × 18½ in.
University Art Museum, University of Minnesota, Minneapolis; Bequest of Hudson Walker from the Ione and Hudson Walker Collection

60. Ferdinand Hodler (1853–1918)
The Mönch in Early Morning Light, 1911
Oil on canvas, 34⅝ × 26 in.
Private collection

OPPOSITE, LEFT
61. *Trees No. 6, 1927*
Pencil on paper,
14⅝ × 11⅝ in.
Hirschl & Adler Galleries, Inc.,
New York

On Cézanne: "'To annihilate myself in the subject—*to become* one *with it*'—this was the purpose of the sweet old man consumed with humility and sincerity. . . ."

the Mediterranean coast; Hartley, typically, sought out the rugged mountain terrain of the nearby Maritime Alps, which appealed to him for its aristocratic sobriety and nobility of design.[23] Always ready for a new vision and fresh start, not wanting to repeat old experiences or old ideas, he worked in Vence for a year, despite disliking the town and yearning for the friends and security of Berlin. He admitted to Stieglitz that it took a long time and much patience "to see over the surface of a place and find the key."[24]

Eventually, in such works as *Purple Mountains, Vence* (plate 40), Hartley found the right key—a pristine clarity of light and pattern. The high vantage point, the rich coloration of lush green, ocher, and purple, and the strong linear design recall the mountain paintings of Ferdinand Hodler (plate 60), a Swiss artist whom Hartley admired and later wrote about as a great painter of mountain "portraits."[25] Other of Hartley's scenes from the same region are equally bold in conception, depicting mountains with sculpted gorges, sometimes crossed by aqueducts or winding roads. In the harsh light even the shadows evoke a kind of black heat.

In March 1926 Hartley went to Paris and saw a Cézanne exhibition at Bernheim-Jeune galleries, which rekindled his interest in the master from Aix-en-Provence. Soon after, he visited Aix and determined that it would be his next locus. Apprenticeship to Cézanne in his own terrain was a logical step in Hartley's pursuit of greater intellectual clarity and objectivity. He marveled that Cézanne was able to see so much in his native region (a lesson Hartley had yet to learn). Immersed so totally and passionately in his subject—whether a mountain, a tree, or an apple—Cézanne was able (as Hartley saw it) to reach a point of detached contemplation where artistic ego vanishes and the object thereby stands for ultimate reality. That Cézanne was, above all, a moral example for Hartley is evident from "The MOUNTAIN and the RECONSTRUCTION," a poem he wrote accompanying a 1928 exhibition of his work, in which he calls Cézanne "the sweet old man."[26]

While in Aix, from 1926 to 1928 (a stay interrupted by a trip to America in 1928 and jaunts to London, Paris, and Germany), Hartley lived and worked in the heart of Cézanne territory—first in a little house called "Song of a Cricket" and later near the Château Noir in Maison Maria, which Cézanne at one time had used as a second studio (plate 62). In these temporary homes Hartley did his own housekeeping, walking several miles into Aix for provisions once or twice a week. Here also he found the freedom and right mixture of solitude and conviviality for productive work. In the company of a few American and French friends, occasional visitors, and his dog (a cocker spaniel he adored and the only pet he ever owned), and with periodic trips to Marseilles or Cannes for transient homosexual encounters, he

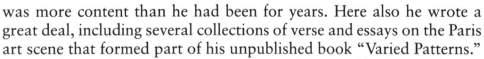

62. Maison Maria, Aix-en-Provence, France, c. 1929

63. Marsden Hartley at Aix-en-Provence with his dog, Toy, 1928

was more content than he had been for years. Here also he wrote a great deal, including several collections of verse and essays on the Paris art scene that formed part of his unpublished book "Varied Patterns."

So devoted was Hartley to studying Cézanne that he sought out many of the motifs in Cézanne's paintings and made numerous pencil and silverpoint drawings of trees and rocks in the forest near the Château Noir. *Trees No. 6* (plate 61), with its complex pattern of intertwining branches and trunks, harks back to such Maine paintings as *Landscape No. 16* (plate 8). In these drawings and in oils such as *Fig Tree* (frontispiece), Hartley was searching for the design *beneath* the surface appearance, trying, as he later wrote, to make something

64. *Landscape No. 29, Vence*, 1925
Oil on canvas, 19½ × 24 in.
Michael St. Clair, Babcock
Galleries, New York

"happen to us so that they [the trees and sky] take on what we never before."[27] In *Fig Tree* we do indeed see a tree as if with "first sight." The bare, ghostly branches silhouetted against the green-black sky, the foreground aflame with orange shrubs create a raw, primordial setting that would reemerge in later scenes of driftwood configurations on Maine rivers (plate 114).

Landscape No. 29, Vence (plate 64) takes the same vantage point as Cézanne's *Mont Sainte-Victoire and Château Noir* (plate 65).[28] Here Hartley's painting method has shifted from the dense flat colors of *Purple Mountains, Vence* to broad parallel strokes that emulate the

65. Paul Cézanne (1839–1906)
Mont Sainte-Victoire and Château Noir, 1904–6
Oil on canvas, 26 × 32⅜ in.
Bridgestone Museum of Art,
Ishibashi Foundation, Tokyo

facture invented by Cézanne as a way of defining mass by means of color harmonies. Hartley also used the unpainted white of the canvas to aerate the space, a technique he had first adopted from Cézanne in the 1912–13 Musical Theme paintings.

William Agee points out that Hartley had a richer and more complex relationship to Cézanne than most artists who turned to the French master's work during this critical postwar period. Hartley's assimilation of Cézanne's method was "so literal," Agee writes, "that the originality of these paintings reveals itself slowly. They are, to be sure, an act of homage, but the results are startling. The touch is rougher, the image more condensed, the contrasts often sharper than those found in Cézanne; but finally it is the range of hue and the range of light effects that makes these works so original and such marvels of the art of painting." [29]

Hartley's view of Mont Sainte-Victoire emerges from blocks of color rather than from a buildup of small parallel strokes, as in Cézanne. In *Mont Sainte-Victoire, Aix-en-Provence* (plate 66; seen from the Tholonet Road, as in Cézanne's version of the motif in the Hermitage Museum[30]), Hartley's forms are more bold and solid, the color more distinctly hot (in mountain, sky, and road) or cool (in the green-black forested areas) than one would find in Cézanne. The heightened color, with its acid yellow and hot pinks, actually draws more from van Gogh's visionary landscapes of southern France.

66. *Mont Sainte-Victoire, Aix-en-Provence,* 1927
Oil on canvas, 25½ × 31⅞ in.
Mr. and Mrs. Carl D. Lobell

The Mont Sainte-Victoire paintings must be viewed in the larger context of Hartley's career as a great painter of mountains. He was intrigued by Cézanne's obsession with "his" mountain. The only insightful article written about Hartley's works from Aix when they were first shown in New York argued that although they seem at first "almost arrogant, a little inaccessible," these views of Mont Sainte-Victoire "are not cold, but their warmth is not of the surface. It lies in depth and density. The strongest colors are not of the exterior; they come, it seems, from behind the canvas, from an internal flame which multiplies their intensity."[31]

In 1928 Hartley spent eight months in the United States, but despite an exhibition in Chicago and travel in the West—to say nothing of pressure from all sides to terminate his long sojourn abroad—he was still not ready to come home. Through the "gentle influences" of the sculptor Gaston Lachaise and his wife, Isabel, with whom he stayed for several weeks in Georgetown, Maine, however, he found what he called "a perfect re-introduction to my native land."[32] America in 1928 was awash in a tide of Regionalist painting and cultural isolationism. Waldo Frank, Henry McBride, and Paul Rosenfeld all wrote critically of the American expatriate artists and writers, including Hartley.[33] But Hartley himself deplored the state of French art in the mid-1920s as crassly commercial, repetitious, and superficial.[34] Refusing to accept status as an expatriate, he claimed to be in Provence because it offered him the same solitude it had offered Cézanne; it was a spot where art was not incessantly talked about but done quietly. "They want Americans to be *American,*" Hartley wrote, "and yet they offer little or no spiritual sustenance for their growth and welfare."[35]

When Hartley returned to Paris in August 1928, he was weighed down by the depressing burden of criticism from the home front. He had brought with him from Georgetown a collection of seashells, which he began portraying in still lifes as, he claimed, "a symbol of peace" for his troubled psyche, and to get his "almost paralyzed hand and eye back into health" after not painting for almost a year.[36] As Meyer Schapiro has pointed out with his usual perspicacity, an artist often paints still life "as a calming or redemptive task, a means of self-discipline and concentration; it signifies to him the commitment to the given, the simple and dispassionate—the impersonal universe of matter"[37]—a precise explanation of Hartley's motives and aims at this difficult juncture.

In Paris he painted every day, beginning punctually at noon to get the best of the wan winter light. Gradually he worked the color up to a point of pearlescent luminosity (plate 67). Using broad parallel strokes, Hartley applied thin layers of rich color to achieve the deep blue shadow-aura surrounding the two shells. He was pleased with his new color adjustments, and rightly so. The painting conveys more than the simple image of two shells. Schapiro concludes the above passage by stating that although objects in a still life may be commonplace in appearance, they "become in the course of that contemplation a mystery, a source of metaphysical wonder. Completely secular and stripped of all conventional symbolism, the still-life object, as the meeting-point of boundless forces of atmosphere and light, may evoke a mystical mood like Jakob Boehme's illumination through the glint on a metal ewer."[38]

In *Still Life: Blue Bottle, Orange, and Lemons* (plate 68), both bottle and fruit seem to nestle firmly into the pink ground yet simul-

"New England . . . is like a first wife that one cannot help revering—& yet cannot possibly live with."

67. *Two Shells,* 1928
    Oil on canvas, 19¾ × 24 in.
    Hirshhorn Museum and Sculpture
    Garden, Smithsonian Institution,
    Washington, D.C.; Gift of Joseph
    H. Hirshhorn, 1966

OPPOSITE
68. *Still Life: Blue Bottle, Orange, and
    Lemons,* 1928
    Oil on canvas, 24 × 19½ in.
    Mollie Parnis Livingston

taneously hover in immaterial space. Transformation occurs. We see simple mundane objects, but the translucent color endows them with a clarity and vitality beyond the *thingness* of surface appearance. Hartley also had a penchant for bizarre still-life objects—viney, twisted leaves, hothouse flowers like the anthurium, or exotic (and often erotic) vegetables. In *Still Life with Red Drape* (plate 69), the unusual cast of characters includes a box of garlic cloves and four heads of endive lettuce, which are encircled in the womblike hollow of deep red drapery. The resulting composition creates a compelling, mysterious image against the ambiguous blue ground.

From Paris, Hartley returned in April 1929 to his beloved Maison Maria in Aix, vowing, however, to paint no more French landscapes that would only draw adverse criticism at home (he did finish some of the Mont Sainte-Victoire canvases begun earlier). He was anticipating with both dread and expectation his return to the United States at the end of the year, when his four-year stipend would expire.

Hartley attributed his current problems to his early over-reliance on imagination, and in reading George Santayana's *Skepticism and Animal Faith* (1923) he came to the realization that he must shed the inward-turning subjectivity of the romantic imagination for greater objectivity in both thought and art. He was fond of quoting a phrase from Santayana, "To distinguish that fine edge of truth from the might

of the imagination," as his new aim. Again Hartley gained inspiration from the Christian mystics, most of whom struggled for relinquishment of the mortal ego as the way to gain the state of clarification or oneness with the infinite.[39] The way out of the trap of artistic egocentricity, Hartley found, was through objective clarity, rather than either imagination or intellectuality. The latter, he confessed, "alas is only very roughly indicated in my mental equipment."[40] He disliked the arid intellectuality of the Surrealist painters, whose work he had seen in numerous exhibitions in Paris that winter, and wanted no part of it in his own work. He yearned for an art expression that flowed from the life impulse, not from mental or imaginative sources that had only tenuous connection with life experience. By the fall he felt prepared to face New England again with poise and inner reserve and after traveling to Paris and Germany for a few months, Hartley sailed for home in March 1930.

69. *Still Life with Red Drape*, 1929
Oil on canvas, 18 × 15 in.
Michael St. Clair, Babcock
Galleries, New York

"I want to be life and not myself . . . just a wholesome supply of magnanimous life."

4

EVOLUTION

While still in France and chafing under the criticism that he wasn't painting American landscapes, Hartley had defensively but nonetheless truthfully declared his allegiance to his native New England, "those inviolable elements that never leave one." He also announced his intention "to get into some really wild places" upon his return, because Europe was too tame and had no "savage" landscape.[1] On the suggestion of some friends, he decided on Sugar Hill, New Hampshire, where he went in June 1930. As the summer progressed, it appeared to be the wrong choice. He missed the solitude of Aix and peevishly described New Hampshire as one long boarding house filled with avaricious Yankee hostlers and "scenery hounds [who] look by the mile and see by an instant and have no wish to look deeper." Despondently, he felt he was "doing time or penance" for having been away so long.[2]

In spite of all this, Hartley managed to find those solitary, primitive spots of nature on which his reputation is built. In the Lost River region he discovered deep, boulder-strewn chasms with magnificent waterfalls. *Kinsman Falls, Profile Road, Franconia, New Hampshire* (plate 71) depicts one such spectacle, its boulders piled up in natural disarray. Superimposed over a solid triangular composition of cascading water and upward-tilting rocks is a swirling, free brushstroke in the water areas and straight, tense handling of the rocks. In the forest and the ragged patch of sky, the treatment is more tightly controlled. The artist is in perfect tune with his subject, each natural element discrete in form and feeling. In *Beaver Lake, Lost River Region* (plate 72), a similar density, together with a bold, frontal view, looks back to Mont Sainte-Victoire and at the same time anticipates the later Katahdin series.

After waiting impatiently for the fall colors, Hartley was disappointed by the acrid hues due to a dry summer. Nevertheless, *Mountains No. 17* (plate 73) has a stark, haunting beauty more memorable than typically picturesque scenes of autumn. The exact pyramid of

70. *The Transference of Richard Rolle,*
1932
Oil on backed board, 28 × 26 in.
Lily Levy

ABOVE, LEFT
71. *Kinsman Falls, Profile Road, Franconia, New Hampshire*, 1930
Oil on canvas, 29⅛ × 17 in.
Private collection

ABOVE, RIGHT
72. *Beaver Lake, Lost River Region*, 1930
Oil on canvas, 35 × 30 in.
Walker Art Center, Minneapolis; Gift of Berta H. Walker, 1971

OPPOSITE
73. *Mountains No. 17*, 1930
Oil on board, 36 × 30 in.
Harvey and Françoise Rambach

Moosilauke Mountain had a mystical appeal to the artist. Indeed, in this painting color and design, technique and idea, coalesce in iconic simplicity. Despite an inauspicious beginning, the season's work formed a logical continuum from Aix.

During the following spring Hartley received a Guggenheim fellowship, which provided a stipend for a year of work in a foreign country. He chose Mexico but postponed his departure so that he could return to Gloucester, Massachusetts, to paint a stretch of landscape—a glacial moraine with gigantic boulders called Dogtown Common—which he had discovered on a visit to the area twelve years before. Dogtown would, he felt, prepare him physically and psychically for Mexico. Whereas in New Hampshire he had failed to make a psychological connection with his native New England, at Dogtown the bond was reestablished.

If Hartley's return from errantry abroad had been partially motivated by outside pressures from critics and colleagues, it was definitely

74. *Dogtown*, c. 1934
Black ink on paper,
23½ × 19½ in.
Jon and Barbara Landau

75. *In the Moraine, Dogtown Common, Cape Ann*, 1931
Oil on academy board,
17⅜ × 23⁹⁄₁₆ in.
Georgia Museum of Art, University of Georgia, Athens; University Purchase

On Dogtown: *". . . the place is forsaken and majestically lovely as if nature had at last formed one spot where she can live for herself alone. . . .[It] looked like a cross between Easter Island and Stonehenge—essentially druidic in its appearance—it gives the feeling that an ancient race might turn up at any moment and renew an ageless rite there."*

not a capitulation to the prevailing demand for American Scene painting, for Dogtown was hardly the typical American scene. At first he found it difficult. Lonely, restless, recovering from a debilitating illness that had left him partially deaf, he would go every day and sit among the rocks in this setting straight out of *Wuthering Heights*. Huge boulders—"granite sentinels" he called them—stand eerily against the sky, like dolmens for ancient rites (plate 74). Gradually he began to draw and then to paint, but on the back of one of the first canvases, *In the Moraine, Dogtown Common, Cape Ann* (plate 75), he inscribed three lines from T. S. Eliot's poem *Ash Wednesday* (published the year before), which characterize his own mental and physical situation:

> Teach us to care and not to care
> Teach us to sit still
> Even among these rocks.

He was beginning to realize that his years of searching abroad had been a kind of intellectual wasteland (like that of another momentous poem by Eliot, *The Waste Land,* of 1922), and that his real need was to find a new center, spiritually and geographically, before embarking for Mexico. Dogtown was, he claimed, a "metaphysical" landscape, and his encounter with it was as much mental as sensuous. Struggling in a forbidding wilderness like Jacob wrestling with the angel, he forced himself by isolation and sheer determination to come to terms with himself and with this difficult parcel of land. Hartley stayed in Gloucester nearly six months—until mid-December—and

his letters characterize the experience as reconstructive and evolution-ary. A true believer in the Bergsonian view of art as an aspect of the evolution of consciousness, Hartley once again emerged from a psy-chological or circumstantial morass to press forward into uncharted waters. The bare-branched tree in the shape of a cross in *Mountains in Stone, Dogtown* (plate 76), silhouetted against the blue sky and touching one of the long dense clouds, yet anchored in the rocky ground, conveys the spiritual import of this experience.

Hartley planned a series of small canvases of Dogtown, their modest size a deliberate rebuttal to what he had witnessed in Paris two years before.[3] The great prewar giants—Braque, Derain, Picasso, Maurice de Vlaminck, and others—were, in his view, resting on their laurels, executing large works of diluted Cubism or Expressionism and

76. *Mountains in Stone, Dogtown,* 1931
Oil on board, 18 × 24 in.
Harvey and Françoise Rambach

77. Whale's Jaw, Dogtown Common, Cape Ann, Massachusetts

78. *Whale's Jaw, Dogtown Common, Cape Ann,* 1934
Oil on canvas, 17½ × 23½ in.
Yale University Art Gallery, New Haven, Connecticut; Gift of Walter Bareiss

capitulating to a lucrative commercialism. Rather in the manner of Ryder's seventy tiny paintings, each containing cosmic immensity, Hartley's 18-by-24-inch Dogtown canvases have the density of the stones they portray. Sharply contoured and sculptural, these boulders crop up through the earth's surface as if erupting under the pressure of geological ages. Dogtown had such an impact on Hartley that he returned there in 1934, and then, while in Nova Scotia in 1936, painted a third series from memory.

One impressive formation at Dogtown is an abutment of two monolithic boulders known as "Whale's Jaw" (plate 77), which Hartley rendered many times—in ink, pencil, pastel, and oil. Unlike the minimalist treatment of rocks in his painting *In the Moraine,* the handling in the 1934 version of the Whale's Jaw motif is generally looser, more painterly (plate 78). The graffiti "C.W." and "PEW," ghostly signs left by human visitors, are echoed in the striated lines etched on the wet pigment, adding texture and palpable presence to the rock formations.[4] *Whale's Jaw, Dogtown Common, Cape Ann* completes a cycle of metamorphosis and metaphor: formed originally by elemental forces of nature, the rocks are transformed by the power of imagination into another monolith, the largest living mammal, a sea creature stranded first on a barren field and then on the field of canvas. Charles Olson, poet and longtime resident of Gloucester, saw this metamorphosis in Hartley's Dogtown and later paintings in religious terms, as transubstantiation. In his epic *Maximus Poems* Olson tells us:

. . . what he did with that bald jaw of stone . . .
such cloth he turned all things to,
made palms of hands of gulls,
Maine monoliths apostles,
a meal of fish a final supper
—made of Crane a Marseilles matelot.

Such transubstantiations
   as I am not permitted,
   nor my father,
   who'd never have turned the Whale Jaw back
   to such humanness, neither he nor I as workers,
   are infatuated with.[5]

Olson contrasts the artist's creative transformation of the rock to his father's approach to nature. Like many a Yankee farmer (or modern industrialist), his father, a "worker," "usurped" nature with brute force and "could have split that rock as it is split." The artist, on the other hand, redeems nature through creative transformation—brings it back to human awareness and benign purposes.[6]

Inspired by the chromatic intensity of autumn, Hartley turned to his earlier interest in the correspondence between music and painting. The landscape elements in *Flaming Pool, Dogtown* (plate 79) suggest orchestral cadences: the rocks surrounding the pool are the deep-toned recessionals rising and falling in rhythmic solemnity from the juniper trees which, like organ pipes, are silhouetted against the sky.[7] A series of quick pen sketches (plate 81) and oils executed from memory while Hartley was in Nova Scotia in 1936 (*The Last Stone Walls, Dogtown,* plate 80, and *Green Landscape, Dogtown,* plate 82) depict wild, derelict scenes composed of barbed wire dancing in curvilinear patterns, erect juniper "sentinels," fence posts tilted at contrapuntal angles, and animistic rock piles. It is clear from these pictures that the artist was drawing closer to the final landscape vision that was to emerge a few years later.

Hartley's lifelong reluctance to remain in one locality became, paradoxically, a strengthening factor, forcing him to come to his own unique understanding of place as a state of consciousness. At Dogtown he learned that New England was not necessarily mountains and trees, tourists and Yankee tradesmen; he also learned that place is not a static mental or perceptual construct converted to paint and canvas. Place is the vehicle by which the artist moves out from his own creative center to discern the universal truths of man and his environment.

No doubt his constructive experience at Dogtown did prepare him for Mexico, which he emphatically declared was "the one place I always shall think of as wrong for me."[8] Mexico nearly consumed him, as it did Hart Crane. In April 1932, just one month after Hart-

Soliloquy in Dogtown, Cape Ann

To have come among you, rocks—
not with woodchuck's foraging
* insolence*
where levity of dust so anciently has
* blown*
giving certain lengths and widths of
* plain renown*
where junipers stand thick beside
* you, and*
themselves,
making organpipes for fugues and
* fierce*
recessionals of wind that parry and
* pierce*
the flesh and bone of mortal mind
left to suffer its own windblown
* oblivion. . . .*

79. *Flaming Pool, Dogtown,* 1931
    Oil on academy board, 18 × 24 in.
    Collection of American Literature,
    Beinecke Rare Book and Manu-
    script Library, Yale University, New
    Haven, Connecticut

80. *The Last Stone Walls, Dogtown,*
    1936–37
    Oil on canvas, 17½ × 23½ in.
    Yale University Art Gallery, New
    Haven, Connecticut; Gift of Walter
    Bareiss, B.A. 1940

94

ley's arrival, Crane committed suicide by diving off the ship that was carrying him back to the United States after his own Guggenheim year in Mexico. Crane's suicide cast an ominous pall over Hartley's sojourn in Mexico. He had befriended the poet a few years before and spent the first weeks of his stay in Mexico City trying to stabilize Crane after riotous drinking bouts and at least one other suicide attempt. Hartley had not known Crane well but felt deeply the tragedy of a fellow artist whose passionate sense of art and life touched all those in his wake. Hartley's tributes to Crane in several unpublished essays, a long elegiac poem,[9] and the painting *Eight Bells Folly: Memorial to Hart Crane* (plate 83) attest to his anger and anguish over this loss. He characterized the painting as a marine fantasy meant to capture Crane's madness. The sea and the gruesome shark lunging up as if to engulf the whole ship (possibly a metaphor for the ship of life) represent the cruelty of death by drowning. The sun, moon, and stars probably derive from a line by Paracelsus, the sixteenth-century physician-mystic whose work Hartley was reading in Mexico, "Man is a sun and a moon and a heaven filled with stars." The triangular clouds are partly out of Ryder, partly of mystical significance. The number 33 refers to Crane's age (a dangerous age, according to some

81. *The Old Bars, Dogtown*, 1936
Ink on white wove paper,
10⅛ × 13¹⁄₁₆ in.
University Art Museum, University
of Minnesota, Minneapolis;
Bequest of Hudson Walker from the
Ione and Hudson Walker Collection

82. *Green Landscape, Dogtown*, 1936
Oil on board, 11 × 18 in.
Private collection

83. *Eight Bells Folly: Memorial to Hart Crane,* 1933
Oil on canvas, 31⅝ × 39½ in.
University Art Museum, University of Minnesota, Minneapolis; Gift of Ione and Hudson Walker

occult beliefs). The buoy with the figure 8 (signifying eight bells, or noon, the time Crane jumped overboard) is surrounded by the eyes of other drowned souls staring out of the watery depths.[10]

Despite his ambivalence toward Mexico, Hartley immersed himself in the study of Aztec ruins, temples, and museum artifacts. Influenced by D. H. Lawrence's novel *The Plumed Serpent,* which he was reading at the time, Hartley became intrigued by this ancient culture and its contemporary remnants, people of the earth whose "every face [is] a copy of Aztec sculpture," so different from the Spanish-derived mestizo class, with its animalistic violence, bullfights and bleeding Christ effigies.[11] Hartley found to his delight that in Mexico City "one could have mountains for breakfast lunch and dinner,"[12] and he eagerly anticipated painting Popocatépetl, one of Mexico's highest volcanoes, attractive to him because of its perfectly symmetrical conical shape. Finding the altitude in Mexico City too enervating, he moved in May down to Cuernavaca, where he rented a garage as a studio complete with a view of the volcano.[13] *Popocatépetl, Spirited Morning—Mexico* (plate 84) is one of four versions of the volcano painted, like Hodler's *The Mönch in Early Morning Light* (plate 60), from a high vantage point, almost as if from a nearby cloud, with no ambient landscape, just the naked, triangular essence of the mountain pinnacle. The volcano sits in pristine clarity like an ancient Aztec god.

Hartley's visionary mountain portraits coincided with his continuing involvement with mysticism. In Cuernavaca he had access to a library of occult and metaphysical literature collected by a woman he met there. Besides Evelyn Underhill's *Mysticism* (1911), he read works by Paracelsus, Plotinus, Richard Rolle, and Jan van Ruysbroeck, all of whom he found to be genuine mystics, in contrast to Annie Besant, Charles Leadbeater, Madame Blavatsky, Rudolph Steiner, and various others who were, in his estimation, merely lecturers and writers without true wisdom.[14]

When Hartley's paintings were exhibited at the Galeria de la Escuela Central de Artes Plasticas in Mexico City in February 1933, the

84. *Popocatépetl, Spirited Morning—Mexico,* 1932
Oil on board, 25 × 29 in.
Elizabeth B. Blake

85. *Carnelian Country,* 1932
Oil on cardboard, 23⅞ × 28¾ in.
The Regis Collection, Minneapolis

catalog notes listed them as "Eight Panels for an Arcane Library," perhaps designed to decorate the walls of a private library such as the one he had worked in. Included in the show was *The Transference of Richard Rolle* (plate 70). The painting, as confirmed by the poem on the reverse,[15] is an abstract pictorialization of saintly transfiguration. Rolle, whose "home is in a morning cloud," is symbolized by his initials scattered in the clouds of a sky that is celestial, not atmospheric. The Y probably stands for YSHEU, a derivative of *Jesu* used by Rolle in his poem "On the Name of Jesus." The central golden triangle ascends over the burning hot desert like the traditional apotheosis of

Christian saints. The triangle could refer to the three stages—fire, song, and sweetness—through which mortals come to know God, according to Rolle's famous work, *Incendium amoris*.

Here, in the arid bright light of Mexico, Hartley intensified his palette, dispensing with blacks and browns and returning to the saturated primary colors of the German Officer paintings. Color is used expressively rather than naturalistically in these fantasy landscapes. *Carnelian Country* (plate 85) seems to imply danger, blood violence. The sky has a threatening, unearthly darkness to it. Mark Tobey, who was in Mexico at this time, commented to Hartley that there was danger in the "black" light of Mexico.[16] In its surreal sweeping vista of desert, hills, and sky, and in its mood of dark foreboding, *Carnelian Country* calls to mind the earlier New Mexico Recollections.

Another fantasy, *Tollan, Aztec Legend* (plate 86), is based on the Aztec myth that a great white bird, Iztac Quixtl, was once seen flying over the ancient city of Tollan (symbolized by the temple), its heart pierced with a dart. Finding Mexico impossible to deal with in a direct way as landscape, Hartley resorted to myth, fantasy, and arcane images. He ruefully predicted that his pictures would not be well received in New York but added, as if consoling himself, "Blake would not laugh at my fantasies if he saw them."[17]

The year in Mexico had been a trying experience, for a number of reasons. Crane's suicide; physical problems associated with the food, the heat, and the altitude; dislike of what Hartley perceived as

86. *Tollan, Aztec Legend,* 1933
Oil on canvas, 31½ × 39¼ in.
The Regis Collection, Minneapolis

THE VISION EMERGES

Hartley shared the Romantic artist's dilemma of how to express the ineffable and transcendental without resorting to traditional religious subjects.[1] Like other artists in the Northern Romantic lineage, he found ways to sublimate his spiritual inclinations through landscape or express them through mystical associations. During the last eight years of his life, coincidental in time and causality with his return to New England (including, by extension, two summers in Nova Scotia), he found new answers to this old problem of how to reveal the visionary quality inherent in the natural rhythms of everyday experience. This was a hard-won achievement for Hartley—more so than for his contemporaries Marin, Dove, and O'Keeffe because for him it was a struggle that took place in his consciousness as much as on the canvas. His colleagues faced other types of problems during their careers, but for each of them the basic vision that underlay the art evolved more smoothly than for Hartley.

With the United States in the full grip of the Depression when he returned in 1934, Hartley was forced by necessity to participate in the easel project for artists under the Works Project Administration Act. Chafing bitterly under its constraints, he produced little during the months he was involved. In the summer of 1934 his salvation was again Gloucester, where he resumed the Dogtown series and did a number of sea motifs—variations on the earlier still-life-into-landscape device (*Shell and Sea Anemones, Gloucester,* plate 91, and *New England Sea View—Fish House,* plate 92). He lived in Gloucester because it was near his beloved Dogtown, but he was disdainful of

90. *The Lost Felice,* 1939
Oil on canvas, 40 × 30 in.
Los Angeles County Museum of Art; Purchased with Harrison Trust Fund

91. *Shell and Sea Anemones, Gloucester,* 1934
Oil on board, 18 × 24 in.
Michael St. Clair, Babcock
Galleries, New York

the "art colony" mentality, with its commercially attractive, prettified harbor scenes. He reacted with his own invented motifs: close-focus still lifes suspended in unreal space or in front of telescopic seascape vistas.

In plate 92 opposites of near and far, closed and open, mesh in a tightly controlled web of shape, line, and color. The black outline of the fish-house window becomes a ship in a bottle, its lower edge melting into a sandy shore, a transition space before the distant sea. Interior and exterior come together in the blue and white of sea, sky, cloud, and wave, reflected on the bodies of the two fish. In contrast to this grip on the composition, the actual handling of the paint is loose and free, accentuated by scored hatchmarks (also seen in the Dogtown works of that summer) on nets, piers, and cork floats. In *Shell and Sea*

Anemones thin layers of white and fleshy pink over dark contour underdrawing give the shell its pearly translucence.

Hartley felt that the second series of Dogtown paintings had deep import, but he was aware that they were not particularly salable. Increasingly burdened by the problem of storing unsold works, he reached a low point of depression in the winter of 1934–35. For years Stieglitz had paid his storage bill, but with a rift growing between the two men (caused by Hartley's long tenure abroad and the consequent lack of American subjects), the aging dealer was no longer willing to help. Seeing no alternative, and with a macabre sense of melodrama, Hartley spent his fifty-eighth birthday, January 4, 1935, in a "massacre of the innocents," destroying one hundred canvases and drawings to reduce the bulk of storage. This crisis, intensified by illness and by

92. *New England Sea View—Fish House*, 1934
Oil on board, 18 × 24 in.
Private collection

bitterness about the absence of support for artists in America, produced a tailspin of despair.

Retreating as before to Bermuda for recuperation, Hartley began to paint—in the absence of what he considered stimulating landscape motifs—flower and fish "fancies." He loved the shimmering, mystical appearance of the many species of tropical fish, some of which had the camouflaging ability to change color. In *Thursday Afternoons and—Summer* (plate 93) the rosy ground, pink sea anemone, and pink underbelly of the fish radiate a kind of luminous aura. Bermuda served its therapeutic purpose and gave him, as he told a friend, a perspective on his past and had "driven up to the surface the best work I have done."[2]

With the intention of meeting his friend Frank Davison in Lunenberg, he sailed to Nova Scotia in September, only to find on his arrival that Davison had already left. Having come all that way, Hartley was determined to investigate the area as a place to work. Eventually he discovered Blue Rocks, a small fishing village four miles up the coast; there he found board with a local fisherman and his family, and then moved a few weeks later to live with Francis and Martha Mason on a nearby island, Eastern Points. Charmed by the simple rural life and the primitive coastal setting (as well as by the cheap board of seven dollars per week, with an abundance of lobster and other good food), he felt immediately at home, commenting in a letter that it was easy to "make my social grade in places like this where raw truth counts more than smooth manners."[3]

Hartley was so comfortable with these people that he felt free to engage in a little "Rabelasian humor" with them or poke about in the kitchen while food was being prepared. In fact, it is still a standard joke in the Knickle household (the first family he boarded with in Blue Rocks) to say to anyone lifting the pot lids to taste the contents, "Get out of there; who do you think you are? Mr. Hartley?" This is the Hartley born of working-class roots—the man behind the mask of the dandified sophisticate that he projected to the New York art world. Hartley entered fully into the genial, demonstrative interchange among the men on the island and no doubt felt a homoerotic affection for the two sons, Donny and Alty. But with his typical sensitivity regarding his homosexual activity, he stated quite clearly that he would forego overt behavior in small communities such as Blue Rocks rather than create a stir.[4] Besides, he had too much affection for Francis and Martha Mason to do anything that would jeopardize their respected position in the community.

Hartley's letters from that fall and the next summer, which he also spent there, brim with excitement about the Mason family. He planned to write a narrative based on their life called "Cleophas and His Own" and had already decided on French-Canadian names for

each family member: Cleophas, the father (Francis Mason)—"from him they get clarity and honour"; Marie Ste. Esprit, the mother (Martha Mason)—"from her they get industry and moral force"; Marguerite Felice (Alice)—"the symbol of protection for the family"; and the sons, Alphonse Adelard (Alty), whose thick black hair stood straight up in great tufts, symbolizing his wild, brash energy; and Etienne (Donny)—big and bold in physique but "shy as a thrush."[5] Inspired by the mystic beauty of the parents and daughter and the delightful mixture of jovial masculinity and familial devotion in the boys, Hartley also contemplated a portrait of the family at their evening meal together.

Hartley returned to the Mason home in July 1936, and the sum-

93. *Thursday Afternoons and—Summer,* 1935
Oil on canvas, 14 × 18 in.
Salander-O'Reilly Galleries, New York

94. *Portrait of a Sea Dove*, 1935
   Oil on composition board,
   10 × 14 in.
   The Art Institute of Chicago;
   The Alfred Stieglitz Collection

95. *Labrador Ducks*, 1936
   Oil on board, 17½ × 23½ in.
   Private collection

mer passed tranquilly and creatively. He wrote a great deal and painted a group of "sea signatures," small fauna and other objects washed up on the shore (plates 94, 95); he also produced a third series of Dogtown paintings, this time from memory. In September a sudden hurricane blew in from the sea, and Alty, Donny, and their cousin Allen were drowned in their boat while attempting to return home late at night. Overwhelmed himself by the tragedy, Hartley could hardly bear to watch the grieving parents, yet he was impressed by their quiet dignity in dealing with their loss. He stayed at Eastern Points until December, finishing the poetic narrative "Cleophas and His Own," which now became an elegiac threnody and took on the subtitle "North Atlantic Tragedy."

Hartley's immediate painted reaction to the drowning was *Northern Seascape, off the Banks* (plate 96), a tense and powerful evocation of the merciless violent sea that took the lives of the three youths. As Sanford Schwartz points out, it was Hartley's first Ryderesque painting in twenty-five years.[6] Ryder's vision of man's lonely struggle against elemental nature (plate 14) was a natural source for Hartley to turn to at this moment. The jagged, menacing foreground rocks suggest the same kind of sea malevolence as the shark's mouth in *Eight Bells Folly* (plate 83).

Not until two years later did Hartley begin a series of figure paintings relating to his Nova Scotia experience. That experience—not just the tragedy but more generally the affection and integrity of the Ma-

sons—had remained vividly alive in his imagination, gestating until ripe for release. He spent the summer of 1938 on Vinalhaven, an island off the Maine coast which, with its large fishing industry and "salt-of-the-earth" folk, no doubt reminded him of Nova Scotia. That summer he worked on three figure paintings—his first in fifteen years.

Nova Scotia Fishermen (plate 97), the most narrative of the three, depicts Francis and Donny Mason in oilskins, hunched over their nets in a sleeting rain. The large size of the canvas, plus its handmade, hand-rubbed mahogany frame, and his stated intention to send it to the Whitney Annual that fall indicate that Hartley had calculated the stir it would cause in New York because of the sudden reappearance of the figure and descriptive subject matter in his work. But this was not the beginning of a series of quaint Maine fishing scenes, nor was

96. *Northern Seascape, off the Banks,* 1936
Oil on cardboard, 18³⁄₁₆ × 24 in.
Milwaukee Art Museum; Bequest of Max E. Friedman

97. *Nova Scotia Fishermen,* 1938
Oil on canvas, 30 × 40 in.
IBM Corporation, Armonk, New
York

Hartley about to embrace the "prescribed story or reportorial paintings such as the regionalists indulge in."[7] The solemn faces of the men, their simplified, blocky physiques, and the unnatural illumination that surrounds them remove the scene from the merely mundane. As in *Northern Seascape* the prevailing key is monochromatic; the subject seemed to call for deep crescendos of inky blue, black, white, and steely cold gray.

Fishermen's Last Supper, rendered in two versions (plates 98 and 99), is more a symbolic portrait, a memorial to the family and their lost sons. Intended for enlargement into a mural, perhaps for a fishermen's bethel somewhere,[8] the 1938 maquette depicts the five family members seated at their evening meal in the robin's-egg-blue dining room of the house on Eastern Points. The eight-pointed stars, seen in so many of the prewar abstractions, here symbolize their appointed sacrifice. The word *Mene* on the tablecloth refers to the handwriting on the wall signaling doom to King Belshazzar in the Old Testament for his pride and defiance of God.[9] It was Alty's impetuous bravado—defying nature by rowing home in the storm—that led to their deaths.

In 1940, not having found the opportunity to produce the mural, Hartley executed a larger easel version, which is at once simple and epic. The heavy symbolism of the earlier version has disappeared. Only the laurel wreathes, symbolic of victory over death, and a faint blue aura around the boys remain as quiet signs of death and immor-

tality. *Give Us This Day,* also executed in 1938 (plate 100), is a more allegorical rendition of this theme of Christian communion. The gulls, representing Hartley among the five Masons, partake of the fish.

The Biblical associations and symbolism and the naive treatment in these works are meant to convey the natural humanity of the Mason family as well as the profoundly spiritual implications of their lives of struggle, courage, and sacrifice. Having read the Christian mystics all his life and been impressed by themes of self-renunciation, oneness, and union with the divine, Hartley was constantly torn between his own lack of faith and his yearning for deeper spiritual values. Until he met the Masons he had thought it impossible for a visionary to live successfully in the modern world, with its mechanistic lifestyle and

98. *Fishermen's Last Supper,* 1938
Oil on academy board, 22 × 28 in.
Private collection

"These people have that sort of in-candescence which is peculiar to those who know the meaning of sim-plicity & humility. They are illumined from within which makes them essen-tially mystical in their sense of life."

Fishermen's Last Supper

For wine, they drank the ocean—
for bread, they ate their own
*   despairs;*
counsel from the moon was theirs
for the foolish contention.

Murder is not a pretty thing
yet seas do raucous everything
to make it pretty—
for the foolish or the brave,
a way seas have.

99. *Fishermen's Last Supper,* 1940–41
   Oil on board, 29⅞ × 41 in.
   Roy R. Neuberger

materialistic pursuits. Francis and Martha Mason, as natural mystics, affirmed for him this possibility.

Significantly, the third figure painting Hartley did that summer on Vinalhaven was a portrait of Ryder (plate 101)—another visionary misplaced in the modern world. Portrayed in his rough wool coat and cap, peering shyly out of eyes that seem to see other worlds, Ryder appears out of the night shadows, as Hartley remembered him walking the streets of lower Manhattan in the moonlight. The earth-warm tones that harmonize in flesh, beard, and coat illumine the picture with the same mystical light Hartley admired in Ryder's works. But unlike Ryder, who suffered neglect for his vision, Hartley felt the Masons were somehow able to "maintain an enviable balance between the

material & spiritual worlds [so] that they symbolize for me the term, ideal."[10]

The consciously primitive anatomy of his "archaic" portraits, as Hartley called them (plates 90, 102–4), bring to mind early Greek *kouros* and *kore* figures—with broad shoulders, tapering torsos, and chiseled facial features—as well as their squarely frontal posture and staring eyes. Thick working people's hands lie quietly folded. Cleophas holds a rose (of mystical significance), while Adelard sports one jauntily over his ear.[11] Felice sits solemn and sad—like a figure on a Greek stele guarding the ghostly images of the two brothers behind her. Austere simplicity, stripped even of narrative context, imbues these portraits with the "buddhistic nobility" that Hartley admired in Piero's work.[12] Stylistically they can also be compared to Mexican mural paintings, to Piero's large, mannish females, to works by Georges Rouault, and to Fayum funerary portraits, yet such a diversity of possible sources points conversely to their uniqueness.[13]

Nova Scotia was the final plank in the bridge that brought Hartley back to Maine for the last seven years of his life. He had been skirting its edges since 1930—first in New Hampshire, then Dogtown, and finally Nova Scotia. He had proclaimed his return (somewhat prematurely) in the 1932 poem "Return of the Native" and reiterated it in the famous statement, "On the Subject of Nativeness: A Tribute to Maine" (which was printed in the catalog for his last exhibition with Alfred Stieglitz at An American Place gallery in 1937). Despite the fact that he unabashedly declared himself to be "the painter from Maine," the exhibition itself contained not one painting of Maine.

Hartley's longstanding resistance to Maine stemmed in part from childhood memories of abandonment and his lonely struggles as an aspiring young painter. Having found no nourishment in Maine for his artistic pursuits, he had ventured beyond its limits to gain a measure of success in New York and more congenial and progressive circumstances abroad. To come back entailed the risk of *not* being recognized as a native son who had made good. Indeed, this proved to be the case. No matter how loudly Hartley sounded his own trumpet, he received little attention in his own state during his lifetime.[14] Moreover, he continued to resist being categorized as a Regionalist painter, wanting no part of the reactionary stance taken by critics such as Thomas Craven and artists such as Thomas Hart Benton, who vociferously rejected modernism as un-American. Hartley saw no relation between the chauvinism of "cornbelt" painting and his own brand of localism.

Conceding, however, the need to reestablish himself in America, he knew the logical place was his native region.[15] But having broadened his aesthetic horizon on European modernism and the visionary spirit of the Stieglitz ethos, he felt impelled to state his own terms for

"Who would waste time thinking of the Italianism of Leonardo? The creative spirit is at home wherever that spirit finds breath to draw. It is neither national or international."

ABOVE, LEFT
105. *Birds of the Bagaduce,* 1939
Oil on academy board, 28 × 22 in.
Butler Institute of American Art,
Youngstown, Ohio

ABOVE, RIGHT
106. *Islands, Penobscot Bay,* 1939
Oil on academy board, 10 × 14 in.
Jon and Barbara Landau

OPPOSITE
107. *Camden Hills from Baker's Island,
Penobscot Bay,* 1938
Oil on academy board,
27½ × 21⅝ in.
Stedelijk Museum, Amsterdam

localism. Instead of the nostalgia and sentimentality underlying much Regionalist painting, he proposed to paint the tall trees and granite of Maine not because they were handsome scenery, but "because in them rests the kind of integrity I believe in and from which source I draw my private strength both spiritually and esthetically."[16] Thus, from 1937 until Hartley's death in 1943, Maine became the locus but not the boundary of his vision. Its rockbound coast, its sea and sea creatures, its interior woods dominated by Mt. Katahdin, and its people became his subjects. But, as always with Hartley, the content of those pictures goes deeper than subject—far deeper than mere geography.

From 1937 to 1943 the artist spent about nine months a year in Maine, living with friends or in rented quarters but never settling in his own home (even though by 1940 he had modest funds). The rest of the year he would stay in New York or visit relatives in Cleveland. Hartley found a measure of quietude and centeredness in Maine, but at times he still squirmed under the mental insularity and starkness of the life, hoping to "swing out again" to the Southwest or Europe. This peculiarly American restlessness had as much to do with his creative spirit as with his life circumstances. To move on meant not becoming trapped in a comfortable, repetitive mode. More fully than ever before, he was aware of the inseparable link between art and life that had impelled his art from the beginning.

Georgetown and West Brookville (where Hartley stayed in 1937 and 1939) were quiet littoral communities, located on peninsulas at

the mouths of rivers where land and sea meet, offering abundant pictorial material. Hartley's subjects included island-dotted bays (plates 105–7), tranquil tidal inlets (plate 108), and rocky coasts (plates 109–11). Seascapes were new to Hartley's repertoire (except as they had figured, incidentally, in the view-through-a-window still lifes), but there is nothing tentative or experimental about them. In a kind of spontaneous combustion, they emerged with measured fullness and sensuous appeal. *Fox Island, Georgetown, Maine* (plate 111), for example, has the physicality that Hartley had long admired in the work of Pierre-Auguste Renoir. Shaped with heavy black outlines, the rocks in *Granite by the Sea, Sequin Light, Georgetown* (plate 109) are piled high from lower left to upper right, revealing only a corner of surf and island. They are as choppy and energetic as the sea itself. In *The Light-*

"I want the whole body, the whole flesh, in painting. Renoir said that he painted with all of his manhood, and is it not evident."

111. *Fox Island, Georgetown, Maine,*
c.1937–38
Oil on canvas, 21½ × 28 in.
Addison Gallery of American Art,
Phillips Academy, Andover,
Massachusetts

house (plate 112), the whole picture tilts like a drunken sailor, as if detached from its geological foundation. Spray and clouds fuse into billowy atmosphere.

Like the 1936 Dogtown landscapes, these coastal scenes gyrate with animistic life. After experiencing the monumental Aztec ruins in Mexico, Hartley had commented that he would have to train his eye not to see similar deities in the crude rock formations of New England, adding, "It is never difficult to see images—when the principle of the image is embedded in the soul." [17] This principle—the Emersonian notion that the godhead has its counterpart in nature and animates its forms—links Hartley in a tradition stemming from the American Luminists through Ryder and on to the later generation of Abstract

112. *The Lighthouse*, 1940–41
   Oil on composition board,
   30 × 40⅛ in.
   Margaret Burden Collection,
   New York

Expressionists.[18] Surrounded by smaller rocks and crashing waves, the giant boulders in *Fox Island* are, in the words of a poem from the same period, "playing about like lion cubs over / the loins of these stone lionesses."[19] Similar metaphors abound in both pictures and poems—pathetic fallacies that transform a landscape element into a monolithic deity, the back of a titan, a face in the mountain, the jaws of a shark.

Hartley's return to Maine, and particularly his work within the seascape genre, was undertaken in full awareness of the established position of his colleague John Marin and was motivated by equal amounts of respect for Marin's talent (as evident in two catalog essays Hartley wrote for Marin exhibitions in 1928 and 1936) and a lively sense of competition. Hartley more than once suggested his own superior position as a Maine *native* and no doubt felt a degree of satisfaction at having successfully entered Marin's turf after so long abroad. Marin's work had always sold well; now for the first time Hartley's was receiving its due. His Nova Scotia experience had given him intimate knowledge of the sea's malevolence, which he now applied to numerous portrayals of hurricanes, storms, and their aftermath along the coast of Maine. In fact, Marin and Hartley must have witnessed and painted many of the same coastal hurricanes, as in 1938, when Marin executed *After the Hurricane, Cape Split, Maine*[20] and Hartley, *After the Storm* (plate 113). The distinguishing factor between the two sensibilities is the proportion of rock to water: Ma-

113. *After the Storm*, 1938
Oil on canvas, 30 × 40⅛ in.
The Portland Art Museum,
Portland, Oregon;
Ella M. Hirsch Fund

114. *Driftwood on the Bagaduce*,
1939
Oil on canvas, 30⅛ × 40⅛ in.
The Saint Louis Art Museum;
Gift of Morton D. May

rin's scene is about eighty percent water; Hartley's is largely rock. In Marin's raucous, turbulent sea is seen his superb gift for capturing movement. Hartley's focus is more on the rocks than the waves.

After the Nova Scotia tragedy Hartley had done at least six versions of stormy seas showing no shoreline, only a lone ship; but they are all small works—studies, perhaps, for *Northern Seascape* (plate 96). Even in a picture such as *The Wave* (plate 110), where the action of the water is central, the wave takes on the monumentality of a Dogtown boulder. For Hartley, liquid and solid forms were almost interchangeable; as elemental forces they are at once time (duration of the moment) and eternity, like T. S. Eliot's "still point of the turning world." At West Brookville, Hartley found equally dramatic subjects among the great heaps of driftwood along the river selvages. In *Driftwood on the Bagaduce* (plate 114) sun-bleached logs writhe like a giant sea serpent, its sinuous limbs searching the air like tentacles. A similar mood pervades his paintings of inland scenes such as *West Brookville, Maine* (plate 115), in which felled trees piled in two angled

LEFT
115. *West Brookville, Maine*, 1939
Oil on academy board, 22 × 16 in.
The Equitable, New York

PAGE 128
116. *Smelt Brook Falls*, 1937
Oil on board, 28 × 22 in.
The Saint Louis Art Museum; Purchase, Eliza McMillan Fund

PAGE 129
117. *Summer, Sea, Window, Red Curtain*, 1942
Oil on panel, 40 × 30 in.
Addison Gallery of American Art, Phillips Academy, Andover, Massachusetts

rows create a kind of dance pattern accented by stumps and erect, uncut trees.

Maine had a freeing effect on Hartley, unleashing his full expressionist potential and enabling him to portray a quintessential summer day on the coast as impressively as its threatening seas. In *Summer, Sea, Window, Red Curtain* (plate 117), for instance, the combination of still life and sea reappears, uniting the best of Hartley's gifts. The dark cool interior with book, fruit, and flowers is a harmony of deep red, orange, and gold, while the blue-gray vase links interior and exterior. The view of the sea is limited, framed by the window and thus humanized and made rational, yet the tonal contrasts draw the viewer outward to the seductively sun-flicked ocean surface, then to the great white cloud, floating like a luminous rectangle by Mark Rothko. The moment portrayed in this work is the existential point of contact between the intimately familiar and the distant unknown.

In October 1939 came the single most important event of Hartley's years in Maine: his long-desired trip to Mt. Katahdin. He knew from various sources that the only view worth painting was from the northeast, near Katahdin Lake, where the mountain takes on the sharply conical form he had always favored for his mountain compositions (the more common and accessible view shows the whole range broadside). The trip entailed numerous difficulties, including a trek in cold rain through deep woods. Caleb Scribner, a Maine state game warden, escorted him to Cobbs Camp and left him there for eight days. The cabins such as the one he sketched (plate 118) were rough-hewn log huts, the cracks stuffed with moss, and with only a small stove for heat. This was a bracing experience for the sixty-two-year-old artist, who was not in robust health nor used to backwoods conditions.[21] It was Caleb Scribner as much as the mountain that gave meaning to the whole endeavor. The two men established an immediate rapport. Hartley was deeply impressed by Scribner's sensitive devotion to the pilgrimage and by his "rare sense of the 4th dimensional sense of plain experience."[22] Like the Masons in Nova Scotia, Scribner possessed vast practical knowledge (in his case, of Katahdin and wilderness life) and an intuitive sense of life's deeper values.

The weather was cold but generally clear, enabling Hartley to study the mountain at length and to do many drawings plus a couple of oil sketches. The view of Katahdin in these drawings (plate 119) and later in virtually all the paintings is a simple one: the triangular mountain rising up from the base of the lake (plates 121–23). Hartley's modifications of the view are minimal; he elevated the viewpoint and slightly foreshortened the middle ground.

Over the next three years Hartley did around eighteen versions of the mountain. Having experienced it factually, face-to-face, he then stepped away from this intimacy—as he had in New Mexico, Dog-

121. *Blue Landscape,* 1942
Oil on canvas, 16 × 20 in.
The Equitable, New York

town, and Nova Scotia—and, with the liberating freedom of imagination and memory, executed paintings using the same basic format
but with seemingly endless expressive variation. The simplicity of the
scene with its iconic gestalt image lent itself naturally to this kind of
thematic serialization. Like the different voices in a fugue, the four
landscape elements of lake, middle ground (accented by the two tow-
ering, gracious sentinel pines), mountain, and sky constitute an intrin-
sic compositional unity from which arise a rich interplay of melodies.
In *Blue Landscape* (plate 121) naturalism gives way to severe simpli-
fication of contour and bold color. Deep mystic blue, counterbalanced
by harmonizing shades in lake and sky, contrasts with the warm gold
and orange of the fall undergrowth. In *Mount Katahdin, Maine, First
Snow, No. 1* (plate 122), the mountainside is scored with deep cre-
vasses defined by black outlines against a light covering of snow.[23]

Hartley was familiar with Thoreau's famous account in *The
Maine Woods* of his encounter with the mountain—this "primeval,
untamed, and forever untameable *Nature*." On this alien ground the
sage of Walden Pond (a tame wilderness by comparison) had con-

122. *Mount Katahdin, Maine, First Snow, No. 1*, 1939–40
Oil on board, 22 × 28 in.
Private collection

fronted the sublime existential questions: "rocks and trees, wind on our cheeks! the *solid* earth! the *actual* world! the *common sense*! *Contact*! *Contact*! Who are we? where are we?"[24] Thoreau, having climbed to the summit, stood among the cloud-enshrouded gray granite boulders, face-to-face with brute nature which challenged his very identity in time and place, defying common sense and human contact.

Unlike Thoreau, Hartley did not climb Katahdin, but even from the relative security of the isolated lakeside at its base, he was no less impressed by its physical grandeur. He experienced the mountain from the pinnacle of a hard-won career as an artist and, perceiving it primarily as form, was able to do for the mountain what Thoreau could not—"turn it," in Olson's words, "to such humanness." Hartley, like Thoreau, wrote of the mountain in terms of its thingness, its geological presence, but as an artist he interpreted it in terms of creative reduction: the grandeur of the mountain becomes "an image of the world in the mind."[25] It is given context in human consciousness (the artist's imagination) and thereby "tamed"—brought to understanding.

From the linear, hard-edged sobriety of the 1939 canvases, the

123. *Mount Katahdin*, 1941
Oil on Masonite, 22 × 28 in.
Mrs. Paul J. Schrag

Katahdin series progressed to the sheer poetic lyricism of color-form harmonies (plate 123). Hartley could say after finishing one of these canvases: "I really had a grand time doing it. I really love to paint."[26] All the tentativeness and overt symbolism of his other mountains—Mont Sainte-Victoire, Popocatépetl, the Alps—have given way to the moment of mastery when the experiential meaning of *mountain* has been thoroughly internalized, and only the perfectly expressed image remains.

In this process of internalizing his mountain experience, Hartley came to resemble, as he himself had observed before, the image he was portraying. The mountain pictures, like the rocky coastal scenes and even the still lifes, are, in Sanford Schwartz's term, "veiled self-portraits."[27] As Hartley fulfilled his lifelong aim "to do the mountain's portrait," the metaphor of man as mountain/mountain as man achieved a fluid interchangeability: Ryder's "shaggy eyebrows . . . were like lichens overhanging rocks of granite"; a *Boy in Red, Reading* (plate 124) sits hunched like a giant red hill against a blue sky.[28] Potent with physical energy, *Madawaska—Acadian Light-Heavy* (plate 125), which was executed at the same time as the first Katahdin paintings, is as statuesque and iconic as Ryder or Cleophas or Katahdin. His monumental frame, glowing with an inner heat, fills the canvas, tracing, like the mountain contours, blocky geometric patterns in arms, torso, and head.

Hartley's Nova Scotia experience was the catalyst liberating the figure in his work. In the Masons he had found the exact measure of mystic humanism to inspire a whole series of figure paintings in his final years. Fishermen (plates 97 and 127) are so totally in and of their natural setting that they almost meld with the landscape. Muscular

124. *Boy in Red, Reading,* 1941
Oil on board, 22 × 28 in.
Mr. and Mrs. Carl D. Lobell

French-Canadians, on the other hand (plate 129), loom like giants, sitting or striding forward on Old Orchard Beach in silent homage to Cézanne's *Bather* (plate 128). Hartley's young lumberjack, like Cézanne's bather, is *on* a ground plane but not precisely *in* the landscape. Both come to life through a combination of traditional modeling (which gives weight and volume to the anatomy) and expressive techniques—black outline drawing and the flat patches of sky between the bent arms—which in turn defy that weight and compress the figure into ambiguous relationship to the ambient space. The result is an

125. *Madawaska—Acadian Light-Heavy,* 1940
Oil on hardboard, 40 × 30 in.
The Art Institute of Chicago;
Bequest of A. James Speyer

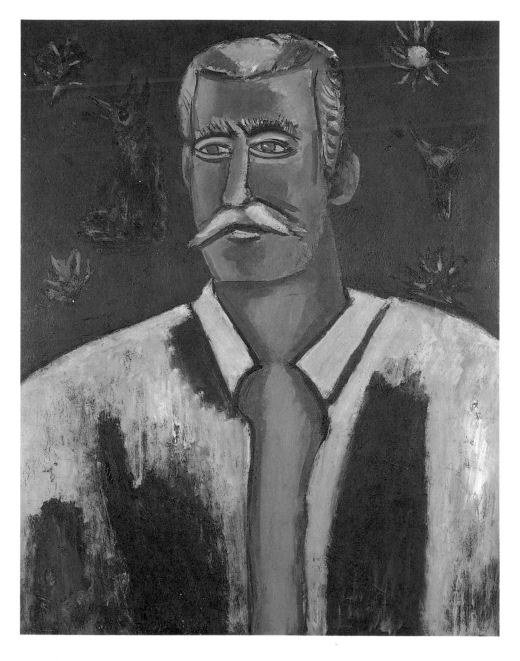

"Trudwell is six-feet-two, looks like a trunk of a redwood, very wide, very square, brawny, big-limbed, with a glorious head topped with silver grey hair, rich vigorous hair that sat about his brow like a sheath of medieval armour, with eyes that looked like pieces out of a November sky, they are so crisp, so brittle in their firm though kindly stare, and as honest as they are brittle."

126. *Arizona Prospector*, 1943
Oil on board, 27½ × 27½ in.
Robert E. Abrams, New York

image with hieratic presence. Hartley's figure is surrounded by a cloud aura; Cézanne's, by a more subtle ether.

Some of the figures, like Ryder, were portrayed from memory, stimulated perhaps by more recent recollections in one of his many essays from the late 1930s. *Arizona Prospector* (plate 126), for instance, portrays a man Hartley met while in the Southwest in 1919–20 and later recalled in an unpublished vignette titled "Story of a Defunct Mine." This prospector, like the wrestlers, swimming champions, and lifeguards, fills the canvas with his presence in superhuman proportion. This befits the heroic role he performs in the story of sav-

127. *Six Lobstermen and Lobster Traps*, c. 1940
Pencil on white paper, 8 × 10⅜ in.
Museum of Art, Olin Arts Center, Bates College, Lewiston, Maine; Marsden Hartley Memorial Collection

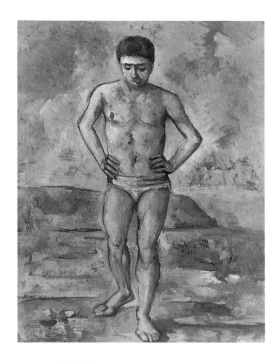

ing the local villagers from a brutal character whom no one else dared to challenge.

Once it was unloosed, Hartley pursued his involvement with the human figure into the realm of religious subject matter, where few artists in an age of advancing secularism dared to tread. Nor did he make it easy for his viewer, with the gawky, giantesque, square-shouldered, small-headed personae who act out his series of pietàs and crucifixions: fishermen holding the body of Christ (plate 130); a mother with her dead son, a bird on her shoulder whispering the bitter madrigal of lament (plate 131); or a pathetic prizefighter and clown who make odd modern companions for a crucified Christ (plate 132).

Like van Gogh, Gauguin, Rouault, and other predecessors, Hartley revived traditional Christian iconography by portraying these religious scenes with twentieth-century peasant-saints. The plain fisherfolk, Acadian heavyweights, and Maine backwoodsmen whom he came to love and admire for their simple verities, defined for him the

BOTTOM
132. *Courage, Power, Pity*, 1943
Black ink on white paper,
10¾ × 8¾ in.
Museum of Art, Olin Arts Center,
Bates College, Lewiston, Maine;
Marsden Hartley Memorial
Collection

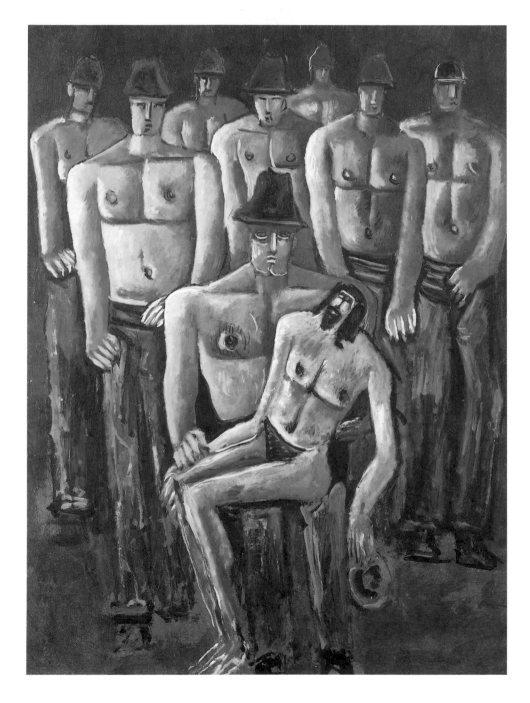

OPPOSITE

133. *Church at Head Tide, No. 2*,
1938–40
Oil on canvas, 28 × 22½ in.
The Minneapolis Institute of Arts;
Gift of Mr. and Mrs. John Cowles

134. *Church at Corea*, c. 1939–42
Charcoal on paper, 28 × 21¾ in.
Salander-O'Reilly Galleries,
New York

Reflex

The macabre simplicity of the white
  church
across the road in which never a
  prayer is
formed nor antiphon sung
seagulls and starlings perching on the
  roof-tree
in hastily devised rows, the tall and
  the short of
it in modified black and white
swallows with sunflush on their
  hearts swooping
up and down the temporal pattern,
  like drunken
punctuation—
July's sentence stiffly spoken against
  August's
too decisive recitation
with its wands of fire-weed if the
  clarion
call has come too soon
are months at times in a hurry to
  get it
over with too—we have known
  them too
who have dreamed too drunkenly.
O whip of any little wind,
drive toward our bleak simplicities
  the
tender thoughts we beckon to us
that we may unarm them in
  unfaltering love.

true meaning of strength, sacrifice, hardship, and virtue. They made it possible for him to deal overtly with the spiritual dimension which, like the yearly crop of granite stones that "grow" in New England soil, emerged periodically in his art when conditions allowed it.

Hartley never ascribed to a church doctrine, though he grew up an Episcopalian and loved the church's ritual. When he chose to paint *Church at Head Tide, No. 2* (plate 133), it was with a complex if not fully conscious intent. Like the empty church in Corea (plate 134), which he sometimes used as a studio, the simple lines, arched form, and monochromatic starkness appealed to his formal sensibility. Barbara Rose sees this choice of subject matter as indicating "an attempt

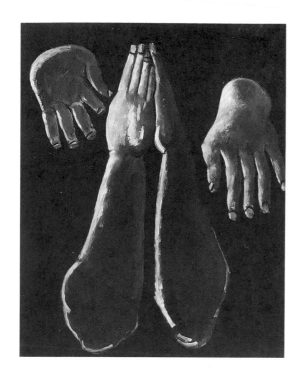

John Donne in His Shroud

It was a smart caprice
to dress
you like this.
Was it a borrowed occasion
as some hire evening suits
for a party?

And the white poppy
on top of your head,
does that mean now white
that it once was red?
For red is the color of a pagan wine
of brisk desire
and of flesh-fire—
white is for calm attire.

In any case, if it is character
is wanted in a face
I would say—look at
John Donne,
that will suffice,
fierce passion turned to ice
and frozen light.

to locate spirituality within the American tradition. Yet the church is abandoned, its black windows shutting out the light of redemption."[29] The church is abandoned because, for Hartley, true religiosity was not to be found there. Instead, in the tradition of American transcendentalism in which he started his career, Hartley perceived a spiritual dimension within the direct experience of nature and in the lives of good and courageous people.

The pairs of hands, thick and strong, that appear out of the darkness in one of Hartley's paintings (plate 135) belong to a workingman. This picture, possibly a study for *Three Friends,* is at once direct in presentation and enigmatic in portent. These hands find their corollary in the series of poems that were among the last Hartley wrote. Titled "Patterns for Prayer," they are dedicated to "One who could not pray" but who yearns for spiritual release and are written in the manner of the fervent verse of Richard Rolle or John Donne, whose portrait effigy Hartley also did at this time (plate 136).

In a 1919 manifesto on the state of modern poetry Hartley had proclaimed, "Poets have work to do for the precision of simplicity, and for the gift of volume in simplicity."[30] The statement also encapsulated his goal as an artist—articulating in words what would take him another twenty years to achieve in paint. After 1919, facing the critical juncture between his years of involvement with European modernism and the postwar abandonment of that nurturing context, he continued his search for a subject large enough to encompass this high goal of volume in simplicity. France, New Mexico, Dogtown, New Hampshire, and Nova Scotia were landmarks along the way.

In the end, Hartley found this volume in simplicity in both large subjects (the pure triangle of a mountain) and humble ones (*Gardener's Gloves and Shears,* plate 137, and *Wild Roses,* plate 138), all of which are unembellished, utterly alone, yet universal in concept. But it was perhaps in the images of dead birds and sea creatures that the breadth of Hartley's vision is most palpably felt. These, too, he considered portraits, rather than conventional still lifes. He had begun these "sea signatures" in Nova Scotia and continued them in Maine. With the voice of an elegiast he recorded the passing of small creatures in both paintings and poems (in these last years the correlations between the two media are numerous).

Hartley was striving to achieve "myopic observation" of detail, the sense of exactitude he found in the work of Jan Vermeer or Willem van Aelst. A *Chinese Seahorse* (plate 139) floats ghostly white against the blue-black waters of its habitat; a granddaddy red lobster (plate 141) lies on a black field. The artist presents his subjects at close range, isolated, devoid of usual still-life trappings of table, wall, or drapery.

OPPOSITE, LEFT
135. *Hands,* 1940
Oil on Masonite, 27¾ × 22 in.
Private collection

OPPOSITE, RIGHT
136. *The Last Look of John Donne,* 1940
Oil on academy board, 28⅛ × 22 in.
The Brooklyn Museum, New York; Gift of Mr. and Mrs. Milton Lowenthal

BELOW, LEFT
137. *Gardener's Gloves and Shears,* 1937
Oil on canvas board, 15⅞ × 20 in.
The Phillips Collection, Washington, D.C.

BELOW, RIGHT
138. *Wild Roses,* 1942
Oil on Masonite, 22 × 28 in.
The Phillips Collection, Washington, D.C.

139. *Chinese Seahorse*, 1938
Oil on board, 24 × 18 in.
University Art Museum, University
of Minnesota, Minneapolis;
Bequest of Hudson Walker from
the Ione and Hudson Walker
Collection

140. *Black Duck No. 1*, 1941
Oil on Masonite, 28 × 22 in.
The Detroit Institute of Arts; Gift
of Robert H. Tannahill

Color is minimal but so concentrated and rich in tonality that the image emerges like a secret treasure from the depths of a dark pool. *Black Duck No. 1* (plate 140), projected forward out of the deepest of black grounds by the whiteness of its wing plumage, is eloquent in its purity. Stripped of the complex iconography of the earlier memorials to the dead—the German Officer paintings or the angry tribute to Hart Crane—this is pure elegy, where form and content coalesce in perfect union.

Hartley's final work is the painting of essential reality, in which what is left unsaid, the profoundly empty space behind the image, conveys as much as the actual subject. Suspended in this Zen-like emptiness are small mundane objects—a bird, a pair of gloves, a duck decoy or lobster buoy—depicted with a deceptively simple—even, at times, ungainly directness. But underneath this American backwoods naïveté was the authority of an artist who had used the European modernist tradition to escape provincialism, and then, with astonishing independence, gone on to become, in the words of one critic, "one of the few Americans of his generation to stand whole and free, at once the undeniable citizen of the world and his own imagination."[31]

For the last three years of his life (1940–43) Hartley spent a good part of each year—from about July through Christmas—living with Forest and Katie Young in Corea, Maine, a coastal fishing village as rough and primitive as Blue Rocks, Nova Scotia. Forest Young was a

141. *Lobster on Black Background,*
    1940–41
    Oil on fiberboard, 22 × 28 in.
    National Museum of American Art,
    Smithsonian Institution,
    Washington, D.C.; Gift of
    Henry P. McIlhenny

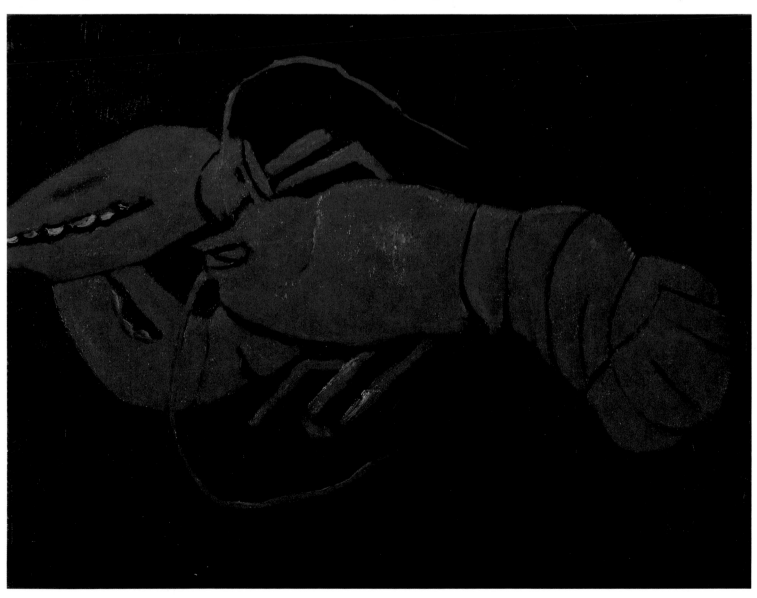

lobsterman, and Katie Young a kindly soul who occasionally took in boarders. They coddled Hartley with good food and solicitous attention, and even took care of him during periods of illness and incapacity, as in the summer of 1943, when his health rapidly deteriorated. On September 2 he died of heart failure in the hospital in nearby Ellsworth, where they had taken him a few days before. Though he had slowed down considerably during those last three years—overweight physically and ponderous in manner—he refused to accept the mental limitations of aging. At age sixty-three he wrote to Adelaide Kuntz: "My work is getting stronger & stronger and more intense all the time. . . . I have such a rush of new energy & notions coming into my head, over my horizon like chariots of fire that all I want is freedom to step aside and execute them."[32] *Roses* (plate 142), the picture on his easel at his death, with its upward thrust of organic life, is surely a work of triumph and joy, not of a dying man.

In 1945 Adelaide Kuntz recalled the last time she saw Hartley. It had been earlier that summer, on a hot day in New York just before his departure for Maine. "He had lingered late in town as if loathe to depart and as if saying many wordless goodbyes. We met by chance in the Museum of Modern Art and I had with me my son, then sixteen, whom he had known from the time he was born, but had not seen for almost a year because the boy had been away in school. Marsden was overjoyed to see him again, and now almost a man, and very formally invited us to dinner 'out of doors on a terrace.' He finally decided to take us to the roof of his hotel, where we dined in the sunset overlooking 'the towers of New York' which he loved. He seemed completely happy and proudly introduced us to some of the inhabitants of the hotel as we went to and from our table. 'Now they can see that I am not just that weird lonely man they have thought, but that I have a family too—May I call you that?' It was infinitely touching to me, especially as I sensed his pride in being able at last, after all the years of fear of spending, to entertain his friends with some lavishness. I shall always remember him like that, with his extraordinary gaze steadfast under the glow of the late sun in his face."[33]

Poet Kenneth Rexroth, who knew Hartley in the early 1920s in New York, summed up his influence on American art as "a moral and spiritual one, rather than literary or physical. . . . That is exactly the moral quality that his personality gave off like a perfume—the true magnanimity which belongs to the very great."[34] Hartley is remembered not only for his remarkable paintings, but also for his humanity, his capacity for enduring friendship, and his struggle with metaphysical issues. Such were the circles of his life that gave largeness to his artistic vision.

142. *Roses,* 1943
Oil on canvas, 40 × 30 in.
Walker Art Center, Minneapolis;
Gift of Ione and Hudson D.
Walker, 1971

"I believe until a man has given up himself he has given up nothing—all his knowledge of accepted aesthetics are of no avail until he has stepped aside from them and given up himself—himself only through the eyes of himself. What a problem everlasting then is it not? A life time of breathless endeavor to be the thing and do the thing of his being—So easy to travel along with claques and crowds, voicing vociferously the great discoveries of each—How ineffably difficult, voicing the soul of one man—alone to himself and—then to whomever else hears. . . ."

IN HARTLEY'S STUDIO

The conventional scene of the artist working away at his easel in a creatively cluttered studio rarely applied to Hartley. Living his entire life in temporary rented quarters, never for longer than ten months at a time, he inevitably had a makeshift studio, varying from the ridiculous (a converted chicken brooding shack in Corea, Maine) to the sublime (the Maison Maria in Aix-en-Provence, which had once been used by Cézanne as a second studio). In 1906, with youthful optimism, Hartley started out his professional career in the traditional manner by renting a studio in Lewiston, Maine, with the intention of supporting himself and this grand space by giving art lessons—only to end up within a year in a deserted cobbler's shop in the backwoods of western Maine.

From that early date on the pattern was established: wherever Hartley's wanderings led him, he would set up a temporary studio in a space that usually doubled as living quarters; sometimes he simply used a spare chair for an easel. Occasionally—as in Nova Scotia, where he used an old fishing shack (plate 143), or in Corea, where he took over the upper floor of a church (plate 144) and later the chicken house—he managed to negotiate separate work space along with his living apartment. Forced by poverty to fend for himself for most of his life, he felt encumbered by the tedium of housekeeping: walking to get provisions and cooking his own meals consumed valuable painting time. In his later years he preferred arrangements where board was also provided (priding himself on his own cooking, he was particular about the quality of food).

Despite (or perhaps because of) his lifelong transience, Hartley managed, once he was settled in a place, to quickly establish and maintain a regular working routine—reading and writing every morning and painting in the afternoon when the light suited his purposes. He was both a prodigious reader and writer, as evidenced by his personal library (now at Bates College in Lewiston, Maine), his three

143. Hartley's studio at Eastern Points, Nova Scotia

144. Church in Corea, Maine, used as a studio by Marsden Hartley in 1940

145. Marsden Hartley's studio (a converted chicken house in Corea, Maine), after his death

hundred essays, his six hundred poems in published and manuscript form, and the enormous correspondence he maintained. He found mental and physical release from the arduous intensity of his painting through these other activities. His reading and writing gave him a wider context in which to view his own art and the work of others and provided spiritual and intellectual stimulus to his painting.

Except for his brief encounter with abstraction between 1912 and 1915, and his late figure paintings, Hartley focused basically on landscapes and still lifes. He tended toward still life when he was living in a city or when he tired of the local landscape. His method of painting still lifes was relatively traditional. He would set up fruit or a vase of flowers, using some favorite piece of crockery (which he collected and would pack up and transport from place to place) and both common and unusual flowers (beach-plum roses, petunias, anthuriums, calla lilies) and fruits or herbs (apples, pears, plantains, cucumbers, garlic, endive). More unusual in both subject and treatment are Hartley's still lifes of fish and crustaceans (crabs, lobsters, sea horses, shells) and of dead birds, which he gathered from beaches himself or which others brought to him. He was not always accurate in his identifications. The bird in *Black Duck No. 1* (plate 140), for instance, is, in fact, an eider duck, and there is no such bird as a sea dove (plate 94).

Hartley's technique as a landscape painter was more complex. In 1941 he stated that because a scene first had to be projected in the imagination and then onto canvas, he had seldom if ever "worked from nature." In other words, he did not consider himself a plein-air or scenery landscapist in the tradition of the Barbizon and Impression-

ist schools. He had to come to terms with a place psychically before he could do anything concrete. His own accounts as well as those of many who knew him indicate that Hartley would often spend hours or days at a certain site in quiet contemplation, without putting pencil to paper.[1] The artist Chenoweth Hall, for instance, relates that she used to drive Hartley to Schoodic Point, near Corea, the site of several major paintings and many drawings (plates 110, 146, and 147); but she never saw him with even a pencil in his hand. He would just *look* at the impressive coast for long periods.[2]

"I have done most of the work," he told Adelaide Kuntz in 1933, "long before the painting begins, and the main job then is to make a 'good piece of painting of it.'" Once the imaginative contact was made and a few key preparatory sketches executed, the canvas became for him an arena where, in the spirit of the circus or vaudeville stage he adored, his "love of the performance for its own sake" could take place.[3] Never having learned to drive, Hartley would tramp long distances to sites that intrigued him—invariably he was attracted to forsaken locations that would appeal to no ordinary landscape artist. Often he would discover only one or two motifs worth painting in a given location. In the Alps, for instance, he found only four views;[4] at Mt. Katahdin only one; and only one or two of Mont Sainte-Victoire. These few motifs he would pursue in series and often in a variety of media as drawings, pastels, lithographs, or oils.

Some locations provided no suitable landscape material at all. California, for instance, had "scenery but no landscape."[5] Many spots (Gloucester, Nova Scotia, New Hampshire, parts of Maine) that would seem appropriate for landscape paintings, Hartley found too pretty or picturesque. His most powerful landscapes were done away from the physical site and richly blend memory with imagination. This was the case with the Dark Mountain paintings of 1909, the New Mexico Recollections, the 1936 memory landscapes of Dogtown, the 1936–38 seascapes of foundering ships on stormy seas, and the late Katahdin paintings. In some instances (in Mexico, for example), lack of compelling landscape would result in fantasy paintings.

Hartley also worked from other kinds of sources. While in West Brookville, Maine, where he was the guest of Clair Spencer and John Evans in 1939, he fretted about the lack of stimulating subject matter. The coast, where he usually found good seascape views, was too far away for him to walk. Clair Evans reported later that to compensate for the lack of accessible seacoast subjects, Hartley borrowed from their living room a book of photographs of Maine lighthouses. Implying that he used this source somewhat furtively to execute *The Lighthouse* (plate 112), she argued that the artist could have painted the lighthouse from the angle he chose only with great difficulty and only if he had been in a small boat. She may not have been aware that

"I have always said that you do not see a thing until you look away from it. In other words, an object or a fact in nature has not become itself until it has been projected in the realm of the imagination. Therefore what has been retained in the mind's eye is what lives. I have seldom or never worked from nature for this reason and so what I see is what I believe to be true, and that becomes the truism of the creative artist."

146. Schoodic Point, Maine

147. *Rock Coast, Sea and Sail,* 1940
Pencil on paper, 8⅛ × 11⅜ in.
Museum of Art, Olin Arts Center,
Bates College, Lewiston, Maine;
Marsden Hartley Memorial
Collection

*". . . Monochrome . . . is the keynote
of the greatest painting that has been
done, from drawings of the cave men
who ground their own colors from
the earth which was composed of
iron, ocher and coal substances, on to
those masterpieces of monochrome
synthesis, the Coptic embroideries, on
up to Rembrandt who was of course
first and last a monochromist. Monochrome is on the whole more livable
and great painters have understood
this, and we see how perfectly the
great masters understood how to
swell their crescendos out of dark
surroundings."*

Hartley had, indeed, sketched the lighthouse on site. Earlier that summer, on the way north to West Brookville, he had stopped off in Portland and sketched the Portland Head Light on Cape Elizabeth.[6] But he
no doubt used the photographic source as well to emphasize the acute
angle of the lighthouse against the wild sea.

Hartley also used photographs as sources for his portraits of
Abraham Lincoln, John Donne, and others.[7] Also, like most painters,
he gained inspiration from other artists simply by pinning reproductions on his walls. In the early years these were often only black and
white, though sometimes he managed to acquire small color prints;
the subjects included works by Cézanne, Piero della Francesca, Hans
Memling, Albrecht Dürer, Jan van Eyck, Leonardo, and many others.
In later years, when he had a little more money, Hartley collected a
few pieces of Egyptian sculpture, Coptic embroideries, and other small
art objects, some of which served as subjects for his poems.

Hartley's role as a draftsman has yet to be fully examined. In fact,
he has often been criticized for his drawing deficiency—particularly in
his late figure work, which has been ignored or scorned for its "awk-
ward" draftsmanship. But like so many painters who could, if they
chose, turn out competent academic drawings (witness the 1923 pastel
figure studies, such as plate 57), Hartley opted for a drawing style as
bold as his painting. This expressive drawing style first emerged in the
1908–9 series of self-portraits (plate 12) and studies of woodcutters
and of seated men and women. These emotionally charged drawings
(particularly the self-portraits) are usually executed in soft pencil, with
a heavy staccato stroke. Later he utilized a similarly rapid, fluid technique with pen and black ink in the 1936 drawings of Nova Scotia
and Dogtown subjects (plate 81).

By the end of Hartley's career, when he had become an established landscape painter, drawings had become an important step in
his understanding and visual grasp of a chosen scene, but his reliance
on preliminary sketches developed only gradually. Other than a few
nature studies of butterflies and flowers, there are no landscape drawings from Hartley's early years. While in New Mexico in 1918, he
began to reevaluate his role as a landscape artist. There—and later at
Dogtown and in the Alps—he favored pastel for its portability and
tonal richness. (He appears to have used watercolor only in still-life
and flower painting; never for landscape.) He took particular care to
have the best pastels and paper and at different times pestered Stieglitz
to send him these materials at his isolated outposts. Unlike many landscape artists, Hartley rarely made any notations of color or light effects on his drawings, though some are inscribed with location, date,
and signature.

The pastels are more like finished works than preparatory
sketches, but in later years Hartley utilized a variety of drawing media

153

and techniques for preliminary sketches. Besides pastels, he usually employed pencil (both hard and soft), pen and ink (both black and sepia), charcoal, and silverpoint for his landscape drawings—with radically different handling for each medium and subject. In contrast to the frenzied pen and ink sketches from Dogtown, the pencil and silverpoint drawings from Aix in 1926–29 (plate 61) and the Bavarian Alps in 1933–34 are highly controlled and refined contour drawings with delicately crosshatched modeling. These latter studies are meticulously rendered observations of mountains, their precision impelled by Hartley's desire to immerse himself in the reality of nature after the mythic and surreal landscape of Mexico. Later, in Maine, when he was striving for monochromatic richness, Hartley also employed a common grease pencil, generally used for marking packages, and schoolroom chalk, a combination that produced a lively tonal contrast.

Whether the preliminary studies were executed with exactitude or flair, Hartley's intent was always to get *inside* nature, to reveal the "psychology" of a given site. Once he felt he had achieved this, the paintings themselves emerged relatively rapidly. Often half a dozen works at various stages of production would be lying around his rented room, but when he was in tune with his subject Hartley rarely belabored the painting process or did much reworking of a canvas. Between 1916 and 1935, when he was under the severe pressure of works that did not sell and a consequent storage bill that he could not afford to pay, Hartley consciously limited his yearly output and the size of his paintings. It was only after 1939, with the encouragement of his dealer, Hudson Walker, that he ventured to increase his overall production and the number of larger works.

Over the years Hartley most often used as support Masonite or academy or composition board; it was less often that he could afford to paint on canvas. During his final years in Maine, 22-by-28-inch Masonite and 30-by-40-inch canvas were the two most common formats of his paintings. When working on the Katahdin series, most of which are on canvas, he complained that he had ruined all his brushes and that "there is no canvas this side of Belgium and Paris that has strength plus intriguing surface."[8] He seemed to favor the hard, strong surface of Masonite, which gave welcome resistance to his vigorous application of paint.

Hartley learned to use the white ground of the canvas to great effect, as evidenced in such works as *The Warriors* (plate 32), which has a decidedly unfinished quality to it. As a transition between the forms, and as unpainted space, the white ground has less physical presence and thus contributes to the mystical ephemerality implied by the subject: the unknown fate of soldiers going into battle. With the German Officer paintings the colors became more intense, but the function of the transition areas of unpainted ground remained the same (plates 37–39). Hartley persisted in the use of bare or white ground during the 1920s when he worked at Aix under Cézanne's influence. Later, in the 1930s, when he frequently used Masonite, he began to exploit the dark liver red of his support ground, instead of the white ground of canvas, giving his late work the deep-toned resonance for which it is justly famous.

After exhibiting Hartley's paintings in his studio in 1909, William Glackens ended up storing the canvases for a long time and later remarked petulantly that in shuffling them around his studio he was "bitten" by one of the thick gouts of paint sticking out all over.[9] As Hartley's work progressed under the influence of Cézanne and Matisse, his use of impasto grew increasingly lighter and the paint thinner, though no less rich in tonality. Hartley, according to his friend Carl Sprinchorn, was able to make a tube of paint go further than anyone else. His Yankee thrift resulted in a painting style that achieved astonishingly rich effects with a minimum of means. Early on he adopted the Post-Impressionist technique (used by Matisse, Kandinsky, Weber, and others) of outlining his shapes in black, and he devloped this technique into an idiosyncratic device for conveying the mass and weight of the landscape forms and figures of his final years.

Hartley's use of color and his handling of paint in the late works from Maine harmonize with his subjects. In the seascapes and coastal views the stroke approximates the activity of the scene: thick white impasto becomes churning water and billowing clouds (plate 110); densely applied blacks, browns, and greens are impenetrable forests (plate 108); rich purples, pinks, and blues intermingle in flowers or mountains (plates 117, 123). Color is always expressive rather than naturalistic and pivots around black and white—either or both of which usually dominate.

Overall, Hartley was an uneven painter. Indeed, at its worst his painting seems to be dead on arrival. At his best, he approached the oil medium with sensuous exuberance, and the results can be breathtaking. In his final years, when the threat of poverty and insufficient sales had lessened somewhat, Hartley was able to give himself more freely to the sheer pleasure of painting. Sometime after 1940 he admitted with uncommon abandon his love for painting: "I am working hard and well these days—finished a 30 × 40 snowstorm effect of Mt. Katahdin yesterday all in one fell swoop and I had a grand time doing it. I really love to paint."[10]

Notes

Introduction (pages 7–9)

1. Herbert Seligmann, "Marsden Hartley of Maine," *Down East* 3 (November–January 1956–57): 26.
2. Marsden Hartley, "Somehow a Past," 1933–c.1939, unpublished manuscript, Hartley Archive, Yale Collection of American Literature, Beinecke Rare Book and Manuscript Library, Yale University. (Letters and manuscripts from Yale hereafter cited as *YCAL.*) See also his untitled poem, "The eagle wants no friends," *The Collected Poems of Marsden Hartley,* ed. Gail R. Scott (Santa Rosa, Calif.: Black Sparrow Press, 1987), p. 101 (hereafter cited as *CP*).
3. *Feininger/Hartley* (New York: Museum of Modern Art, 1944); Elizabeth McCausland, *Marsden Hartley* (Minneapolis: University of Minnesota Press, 1952); Barbara Haskell, *Marsden Hartley* (New York: Whitney Museum of American Art and New York University Press, 1980).
4. Peter Plagens, "Marsden Hartley Revisited or, Were We Really Ever There?" *Artforum* 7 (May 1969): 41.
5. Elizabeth McCausland, "The Return of the Native," *Art in America* 40 (Spring 1952): 77.

1. *The Circle Begins (pages 11–21)*

1. Norma Berger, Hartley's niece, in interview with Gary Gillespie, October 1, 1973, cited in the appendix to "A Collateral Study of Selected Paintings and Poems from Marsden Hartley's Maine Period," Ph.D. diss., Ohio University, 1974.

2. Hartley, "Somehow a Past," YCAL.
3. Ralph Waldo Emerson, *Selected Essays,* ed. Larzer Ziff (New York: Penguin, 1982), pp. 227 and 211. It is not known if Hartley read the first or second series of the *Essays*; there were contemporary editions that contained both in one volume. In his autobiography he does mention specifically "Circles" and "The Over-Soul," both of which are in the first series.
4. Hartley, "Somehow a Past," YCAL.
5. Alice Frost Lord, "Farrar Studio in the 90s Was an Inspiration," *Lewiston Journal,* July 2, 1960.
6. Hartley to Richard Tweedy, November 23, 1900, Hartley Archive, Archives of American Art, Smithsonian Institution, Washington, D.C. (hereafter cited as *AAA*).
7. Hartley to Tweedy, October 25, 1900, AAA.
8. Hartley to Horace Traubel, postmarked October 29, 1907, in *Heart's Gate: Letters between Marsden Hartley and Horace Traubel, 1906–1915,* edited and with an introduction by William Innes Homer (Highlands, N.C.: Jargon Society, 1982), p. 5. It was probably Mrs. Ole Bull who commented to Hartley that his painting was like a passage out of Grieg, since her husband, the noted violinist, Ole Bull, had been Grieg's teacher.
9. Ibid., postmarked February 10, 1907, p. 24.

2. *New and Larger Circles: 291 and Europe (pages 23–55)*

1. Paul Rosenfeld, "American Painting," *Dial* 71 (December 1921): 658.
2. Elizabeth Johns, "Albert Pinkham Ry-

der: Some Thoughts on His Subject Matter," *Arts Magazine* 54 (November 1979): 164–71.

3. On the back of *The Dark Mountain No. 1* are inscribed two notes by Stieglitz, who kept these two paintings in his collection for many years. The first states: "In Mr. Hartley's opinion the finest, most expressive example of his work that year; never exhibited." And a note dated May 20, 1917, says: "I have had this picture before me practically daily for 7 years / I still consider it one of the best of all Hartley's work / It always satisfies me, / It is genuinely Hartley / Significant / Hartley was undoubtedly on the verge of suicide during the summer which brought forth this picture."

4. Hartley to Traubel, postmarked July 23, 1919, in Homer, *Heart's Gate,* p. 72.

5. William Innes Homer, *Alfred Stieglitz and the American Avant-Garde* (Boston: New York Graphic Society, 1977), pp. 152–53.

6. Hartley to Norma Berger, July 11, 1910, YCAL.

7. Hartley noted in a letter to Alfred Stieglitz (July 1911, YCAL) that he was studying reproductions of Cézanne's work; he probably was referring to Julius Meier-Graef's monograph, *Paul Cézanne* (Munich, 1910).

8. Ibid. and Hartley, "Whitman and Cézanne," in *Adventures in the Arts* (New York: Boni, Liveright, 1921; reprinted New York: Hacker Art Books, 1972), pp. 30–36.

9. Gail Levin, "American Art," in *"Primitivism" in 20th Century Art,* ed. William Rubin (New York: Museum of Modern Art, 1985), p. 457.

10. Hartley, postcard to Stieglitz, September 1, 1912, YCAL; Levin, "American Art," p. 456.

11. Hartley was, in fact, influenced by Stein's style. He undertook writing his autobiography, "Somehow a Past," in 1933 after reading Stein's *The Autobiography of Alice B. Toklas.* The cadence and use of repetition in "Somehow a Past" are unmistakable echoes of Stein.

12. *Camera Work,* July 1911. James Mellow, in his biography of Gertrude Stein, *Charmed Circle* (New York: Avon, 1974), pp. 191–92, suggests that the influence of Stein's literary style on the whole genre of portrait abstractions is a subject needing further investigation.

13. William James, *Varieties of Religious Experience* (New York: Macmillan Collier Books, 1961), pp. 319–25. Hartley's account of this painting is stated later in a letter to Adelaide Kuntz (February 17, 1933, AAA), written from Mexico at a time when he was considering returning to the genre.

14. See Lyndel King's catalog notes for this painting in *Marsden Hartley, 1908–1942: The Ione and Hudson D. Walker Collection* (Minneapolis: University Art Museum, University of Minnesota, 1984), p. 22.

15. Hartley to Rockwell Kent, December 24, 1912, AAA.

16. In a letter to his niece, Norma Berger (December 30, 1912, YCAL), Hartley claimed he was the only one doing musical impressions in paint. For discussions of the idea of synaesthesia, and specifically color-music, see Haskell, *Hartley,* pp. 28–29, and Gail Levin, "Marsden Hartley and the European Avant-Garde," *Arts Magazine* 54 (September 1979): 159. For his comment regarding Delaunay, see Hartley to Stieglitz, June 20, 1912, YCAL.

17. Hartley, "Somehow a Past," YCAL.

18. Hartley to Stieglitz, December 20, 1912, YCAL.

19. Hartley to Kent, August 22, 1912, AAA.

20. Gertrude Stein to Alfred Stieglitz, n.d. [April 1913?], YCAL; published in Donald Gallup, "The Weaving of a Pattern: Marsden Hartley and Gertrude Stein," *Magazine of Art* 41 (November 1, 1948): 259.

21. Hartley to Stieglitz, February 8, 1913, YCAL.

22. Gail Levin discusses the climate in prewar Germany in "Hidden Symbolism in Marsden Hartley's Military Pictures," *Arts Magazine* 54 (October 1979): 154–55, where she cites a useful background source: Virginia Cowles, *1913: An End and a Beginning* (New York: Harper and Row, 1967), pp. 58–65.

23. Wassily Kandinsky and Franz Marc, eds. *The Blaue Reiter Almanac,* English translation ed. Klaus Lankheit (New York: Viking Press, 1974), p. 250.

24. Hartley to Stieglitz, n.d. [February 1913], YCAL.

25. Hartley, "Somehow a Past," YCAL.

26. Levin, "Hidden Symbolism," p. 158.

27. Hartley to Stieglitz, October 31, 1913, YCAL. See Gail Levin, "Marsden Hartley, Kandinsky, and Der Blaue Reiter," *Arts Magazine* 52 (November 1977): 156–60, and Levin, "Hartley and the European Avant-Garde," p. 161, for discussions of Hartley's use of Bavarian glass painting.

28. Hartley, "Somehow a Past," YCAL.

29. Hartley to Stieglitz, n.d. [May or June 1913], YCAL. For a different interpretation of this painting, see Levin, "Hidden Symbolism," p. 158.

30. Hartley's statement was reprinted in *Camera Work* 45 (January 1914): 17, and later in Marsden Hartley, *On Art,* ed. Gail R. Scott (New York: Horizon Press, 1982), pp. 62–63.

31. See Levin, "American Art," p. 457.

32. Hartley to Adelaide Kuntz, May 30, 1929, from Mexico City, AAA.

33. The meaning of these emblems and letters is explained in a letter by Arnold Rönnebeck to Duncan Phillips, n.d. [after 1943], YCAL. See also Levin, "Hidden Symbolism."

34. See, for example, Abraham A. Davidson, "Cubism and the Early American Modernist," *Art Journal* 26 (Winter 1966–67): 122–29; and Irma B. Jaffe, "Cubist Elements in the Painting of Marsden Hartley," *Art International* 14 (April 1970): 33–38.

3. *The Search for Clarity* (pages 57–85)

1. Hartley, in "A Word," *Forum Exhibition of Modern American Painters* (New York: Anderson Galleries, 1916; New York: Anno Press, 1968); Hartley's statement reprinted in *On Art,* p. 66.

2. *Camera Work* reprinted excerpts of Bergson's writings, including "What Is the Object of Art?" in *Camera Work,* no. 37 (1912): 25, and "Laughter" from *Creative Evolution* in *Camera Work,* no. 36 (1911): 20–21.

3. *The Autobiography of William Carlos Williams* (New York: New Directions, 1951, 1967), p. 138.

4. Charles Caffin, "New and Important Things in Art: Latest Work by Marsden Hartley," *New York American,* April 17, 1916, p. 8; reprinted along with Hartley's catalog statement in *Camera Work,* no. 48 (October 1916): 59; see also Levin, "Hidden Symbolism," p. 155.

5. Charles Eldredge, "Nature Symbolized: American Painting from Ryder to Hartley," in *The Spiritual in Art: Abstract Painting 1890–1985* (Los Angeles: Los Angeles County Museum of Art; New York: Abbeville Press, 1986), p. 118.

6. Hartley, "The Great Provincetown Summer," unpublished manuscript, YCAL, and "Somehow a Past," YCAL. See also Arthur Frank Wertheim, *The New York Little Renaissance: Iconoclasm, Modernism and Nationalism in American Culture* (New York: New York University Press, 1976), p. 174.

7. Hartley to Stieglitz, September 13, 1916, YCAL.

8. Hartley to Carl Sprinchorn, n.d., McCausland files, AAA.

9. One typical example still owned by Robert Laurent's son, John Laurent, shows tinseled flowers on a black ground.

10. See Sanford Schwartz, "When New York Went to New Mexico," *Art in*

America 64 (July–August 1976): 93–97; reprinted in *The Art Presence* (New York: Horizon Press, 1982), pp. 85–94.

11. For a list of Hartley's essays on the Indian, see *On Art*, pp. 306–7; see also Dickran Tashjian, "Marsden Hartley and the Southwest: A Ceremony for Our Vision, A Fiction for the Eye," *Arts Magazine* 54 (April 1980): 127–31. In addition, see Van Deren Coke, *Taos and Santa Fe: The Artist's Environment, 1882–1942* (Albuquerque: University of New Mexico Press, 1963).

12. "The Festival of the Corn," in *CP*, pp. 62–67. The poem celebrates the Indian corn dance, which takes place on the Catholic feast day of San Domingo. The saint's image is carried through the plaza to the sound of Indian drums and dancing feet.

13. These votive panels were made by the Penitente Brotherhood in a tradition dating back over a hundred years. See Julie Schimmel, "The Hispanic Southwest," in *Art in New Mexico 1900–1945: Paths to Taos and Santa Fe*, ed. Charles Eldredge (Washington, D.C.: National Museum of American Art; New York: Abbeville Press, 1986), pp. 108–45.

14. Hartley to Stieglitz, June 24, 1918, YCAL.

15. For a penetrating reassessment of this issue of postwar retrenchment, see William Agee, "Into the New Century: After the First Wave," in *The Advent of Modernism: Post-Impressionism and North American Art, 1900–1918*, ed. Kelly Morris (Atlanta: High Museum of Art, 1986), pp. 43–56.

16. Marsden Hartley, "America as Landscape," *El Palacio* 5 (December 9, 1918): 341; and Hartley, "Esthetic Sincerity," *El Palacio* 5 (December 21): 333.

17. For accounts of life in postwar Berlin, see Matthew Josephson, *Life among the SurRealists* (New York: Holt, Rinehart, and Winston, 1962); Robert McAlmon, *Being Geniuses Together: 1920–1930*, revised with supplementary chapters by Kay Boyle (Garden City, N.Y.: Doubleday, 1968); and McAlmon's book featuring Hartley as one of its characters, *Distinguished Air (Grim Fairy Tales)* (Paris: Contact Editions, 1925).

18. Patricia Broder, "Marsden Hartley: In Search of American Icons," in *The American West: The Modern Vision* (Boston: Little, Brown and Co.; A New York Graphic Society Book, 1984), p. 131.

19. Ibid., foreword by Charles Eldredge, p. viii.

20. Bram Dijkstra, *Hieroglyphics of a New Speech: Cubism, Stieglitz and the Early Poetry of William Carlos Williams* (Princeton, N.J.: Princeton University Press, 1969), pp. 106ff, and Wertheim, *New York Little Renaissance*, pp. 227ff.

21. Hartley, "Arezzo and Piero" and "Rome and the Ultimate Splendor," in "Varied Patterns," *On Art*, pp. 122–26; see also Hartley's account of this trip in "Somehow a Past," YCAL.

22. Hartley to Stieglitz, April 28, 1923, YCAL.

23. Ibid., October 1, 1925, and December 3, 1925, YCAL.

24. Ibid., February 2, 1926, YCAL.

25. Hartley, "On the Subject of the Mountain: A Letter to Messieurs Segantini and Hodler," in "Letters Never Sent," unpublished manuscript, YCAL. ("Letters Never Sent" was written over the course of Hartley's life as tributes to artists, writers, and friends he admired. They were a self-styled genre of essays in which he was able to address the individual directly and intimately.) The extent of Hodler's influence on Hartley is yet to be explored. Hodler, in fact, wrote an essay "The Physiognomy of Landscape" (c. 1885), which was not translated into English during Hartley's life, but which he may have known. See Jura Bruchweiler, "Ferdinand Hodler: Writer," in *Ferdinand Hodler*, ed. Peter

Selz (Berkeley: University Art Museum, 1972).

26. Hartley, *On Art,* p. 76.

27. Hartley to Kuntz, September 22, 1929, AAA.

28. This scene is definitely *not* Vence, but Aix-en-Provence. The painting does not bear a specific title given by Hartley, but a generic title with a number that was apparently assigned to it at a later date, probably after Hartley's death.

29. Agee, "Into the New Century," p. 48.

30. See *Cézanne: The Late Work* (New York: Museum of Modern Art, 1977), plate 116.

31. M. Debrol, "Marsden Hartley—Painter of Mountains," *Creative Art 2* (June 1928): xxxv; the article was supposed to be the foreword to the exhibition catalog. M. Debrol was a friend of Hartley from France; Arnold Rönnebeck translated her article into English.

32. Hartley to Isabel Lachaise, n.d., McCausland files, AAA.

33. See Waldo Frank, *The Rediscovery of America* (New York: Charles Scribner's Sons, 1929); Henry McBride, "Attractions in the Galleries," *New York Sun,* January 5, 1929, p. 12; and Paul Rosenfeld, "Marsden Hartley," in *Port of New York* (New York: Harcourt Brace and Company, 1924), pp. 83–101; reprinted with an introduction by Sherman Paul (Urbana: University of Illinois Press, 1961).

34. See Hartley's essays in "Varied Patterns," *On Art,* pp. 127–57.

35. Typed excerpt from Hartley's letter to Sprinchorn, n.d., McCausland files, AAA.

36. Hartley to Rebecca Strand, who had also been at Georgetown, January 6, 1929, AAA.

37. Meyer Schapiro, "The Apples of Cézanne: An Essay on the Meaning of Still-Life," in *Modern Art: 19th and 20th Centuries* (New York: George Braziller, 1982), p. 19.

38. Ibid., p. 20.

39. Hartley also read that season Miguel Unamuno's essay "The Spanish Christ," from *Essays and Soliloquies.* See Gail Scott, introduction to *On Art,* pp. 39–42, for an elaboration of this thesis.

40. Hartley to Strand, November 19, 1929, AAA.

4. *Evolution (pages 87–101)*

1. Hartley to Strand, November 19, 1929, and March 6, 1929, AAA.

2. Hartley to Kuntz, July 14, 1930, and to Strand, August 8, 1930, AAA.

3. Hartley to Strand, August 31, 1931, AAA.

4. See Martha Oakes, "Introduction / The Challenge of Dogtown," in *Marsden Hartley: Soliloquy in Dogtown* (Gloucester, Mass.: Cape Ann Historical Association, 1985), pp. 7–10, for the history of Dogtown; and Ronald Paulson, "Marsden Hartley's Search for the Father(land)," in *Marsden Hartley and Nova Scotia,* ed. Gerald Ferguson (Halifax, Nova Scotia: Mount Saint Vincent University Art Gallery, 1987), p. 22.

5. Charles Olson, *The Maximus Poems* (New York: Jargon/Corinth Books, 1960), p. 33.

6. See Gail Scott, "Marsden Hartley at Dogtown Common," *Arts Magazine* 54 (October 1979): 159–65, for a fuller discussion of this subject.

7. On the back of *Flaming Pool, Dogtown,* Hartley inscribed a poem, "Beethoven in Dogtown," which is apparently the first version of "Soliloquy in Dogtown," in *CP,* pp. 175–76.

8. Hartley, "Somehow a Past," YCAL.

9. Hartley, "Dear Hart," in "Letters Never Sent"; "Hart Crane in Mexico"; "Hart Crane, the Life of a Poet," in "The Spangle of Existence"—unpublished MSS, YCAL; and "In Memoriam—Hart Crane R.I.P.," in *CP,* pp. 119–27, 333–34.

10. Hartley to Kuntz, December 5, 1933, AAA.

11. Ibid., March 14, 1932, AAA. See also Hartley, "The Bleeding Christs of Mexico," in "The Spangle of Existence"; unpublished essays: "Mexican Retablos," "Mexican Vignettes," "Tlanepantla," and "The Virgin of Tlaltenango"; and the section on Mexico in his autobiography, "Somehow a Past," YCAL.

12. Hartley to Kuntz, March 14, 1932, AAA.

13. It was at this time that Hartley wrote the essay "On the Subject of the Mountain: A Letter to Messieurs Segantini and Hodler," in "Letters Never Sent," YCAL.

14. Hartley to Kuntz, July 28, 1932, AAA.

15. Hartley, "Richard Rolle," in *CP*, p. 295.

16. Hartley to Kuntz, October 16, 1932, AAA.

17. Ibid., February 17, 1933, AAA.

18. Ibid., June 27, 1932, AAA.

19. Ibid., December 22, 1933, AAA.

20. Robert Rosenblum, *Modern Painting and the Northern Romantic Tradition* (New York: Harper and Row, 1975), pp. 45 ff.

21. Clement Greenberg, *Nation* 30 (December 1944): 810; reprinted in *The Collected Essays and Criticism: Perception and Judgement, 1939–1944,* vol. 1, ed. John O'Brian (Chicago: University of Chicago Press, 1986), p. 247.

22. Hartley to Kuntz, February 3, 1934, and November 4, 1933, AAA.

5. The Vision Emerges (pages 103–47)

1. Although Hartley is not included in Rosenblum's discussion, he nevertheless conforms to most of the patterns defined for this tradition. See also Roald Nasgaard, *The Mystic North: Symbolist Landscape Painting in Northern Europe and North America 1890–1940* (Toronto: Art Gallery of Ontario and University of Toronto Press, 1984), pp. 203–16; and Eldredge, "Nature Symbolized," pp. 118–22.

2. Hartley to Kuntz, August 4, 1935, AAA.

3. Ibid., October 16, 1935, AAA.

4. The Leander Knickle anecdote was related to Gerald Ferguson, who organized the exhibition *Marsden Hartley and Nova Scotia* at the Mount Saint Vincent University Art Gallery, Halifax, Nova Scotia, October 22–November 23, 1987. In a letter to Arnold Rönnebeck (November 8, 1936, YCAL), Hartley contrasted the restricted homosexual behavior necessary in small towns with the freedom they had both enjoyed in the pre- and postwar Berlin periods.

5. Hartley to Kuntz, November 4, 1935, and an undated letter, probably 1935, AAA. See Marsden Hartley, *Cleophas and His Own: A North Atlantic Tragedy,* facsimile edition (Halifax: Nova Scotia College of Art and Design, 1982); reprinted in *Marsden Hartley and Nova Scotia,* ed. Gerald Ferguson, pp. 83–122. See in the same volume Gail R. Scott, "*Cleophas and His Own:* The Making of a Narrative," pp. 55–73.

6. Sanford Schwartz, "A Northern Seascape," *Art in America* 64 (January–February 1967): 72–76; reprinted in *The Art Presence,* pp. 53–63.

7. Hartley to Kuntz, November 17, 1938, AAA.

8. Hudson Walker, Hartley's dealer from the late 1930s, related in an interview with Elizabeth McCausland how he had hoped to have the scene done as a mural on the stairway of the Walker Art Center in Minneapolis. "Hudson Walker's Recollections of the Artist in a Taped Interview," *Journal of the Archives of American Art* 8 (January 1968): 9–21.

9. Hartley was interested in Washington Allston's painting *Belshazzar's Feast* in the Boston Museum of Fine Arts and read about it in a biography of Allston. He admired the Michelangesque

figures and the chromatic richness of Allston's painting. Hartley to Kuntz, August 12, 1931, AAA.

10. Ibid., September 9, 1936, AAA.

11. In *Cleophas and His Own*, Hartley relates an incident when Cleophas ate the petals of a beach-plum rose, after which he seemed to glow with mystic light.

12. Hartley, "Somehow a Past," YCAL.

13. Haskell, *Hartley*, p. 116, and Paulson, "Hartley's Search for the Father-(land)," p. 22. In the late 1930s, when Hartley had a little extra money, he bought a number of Coptic embroideries and a Fayum portrait of a woman, which he greatly admired.

14. Hartley sent photographs of his work and copies of his publications to the state library at Augusta, offered his paintings to the University of Maine, lectured in Portland and Orono, and otherwise promoted himself.

15. See Elizabeth McCausland, "The Return of the Native," *Art in America* 40 (Spring 1952): 55–79, and Vivian Endicott Barnett, "Marsden Hartley's Return to Maine," *Arts Magazine* 54 (October 1979): 172–76.

16. Hartley, "Is There an American Art?" in *On Art*, p. 199.

17. Hartley to Kuntz, April 4, 1932, AAA.

18. See Paulson, "Hartley's Search for the Father(land)," pp. 28–33, for a slightly more Jungian version of this thesis.

19. Hartley, "Listening to the Music," in *CP*, p. 228.

20. A number of the seascapes were purchased quickly by prominent museums and for higher prices than his work had ever commanded. The Worcester Art Museum, Worcester, Massachusetts, purchased *The Wave* in 1941; the Whitney Museum of American Art, New York, bought *Granite by the Sea* in 1942; the Portland [Oregon] Museum bought *After the Storm* in 1941; and the Addison Gallery of American Art, Phillips Academy, Andover, Massachusetts, bought *Fox Is-land, Georgetown, Maine* soon after it was painted. For a reproduction of Marin's *After the Hurricane, Cape Split, Maine,* see Sheldon Reich, *John Marin Catalogue Raisonné*, vol. 2, (Tucson: University of Arizona Press, 1970), p. 694 (38.29).

21. The path Hartley took through the woods is still the only access to the camp other than a seaplane. The camp is still in operation and has changed little since 1939.

22. Hartley to Kuntz, October 24, 1939, AAA.

23. Hartley's accounts of the trip indicate that there was a light snowfall while he was there, but that he also planned to visit Scribner in Patten for Christmas to paint the mountain in winter snow. Due to illness Scribner could not accommodate him, so the four snow versions of Katahdin probably sprang as much from Hartley's imaginative projections as from observation. Two of these snow scenes depict a wild, swirling snowstorm reminiscent of the 1908–9 blizzard scenes.

24. Henry David Thoreau, *Ktaadn* (New York: Tanam Press, 1980), pp. 78–80.

25. Hartley, "On the Subject of the Mountain," YCAL. See also Hartley's poems "The MOUNTAIN and the RECONSTRUCTION," in *On Art*, pp. 74–77, and "The Pilgrimage and the Game Warden," in *CP*, pp. 245–46.

26. As recorded in a letter to George (unidentified) in the McCausland files (roll 272, frame 802), AAA.

27. Schwartz, "Northern Seascape," p. 73.

28. Hartley, "Albert Pinkham Ryder," in *On Art*, p. 261. Is it possible that *Boy in Red, Reading* inspired Wallace Stevens's poem "Large Red Man Reading"? Stevens had been involved with modern art since the 1920s and wrote other poems after paintings by Hartley's contemporaries.

29. Barbara Rose, *American Painting: The Twentieth Century* (New York: Skira/Rizzoli, 1986), p. 19.

30. Hartley, "On the Business of Poetry," in *CP*, p. 315.

31. Jerome Mellquist, "Marsden Hartley," *Perspectives U.S.A.*, no. 4 (Summer 1953): 77.

32. Hartley to Kuntz, February 2, 1940, AAA.

33. Adelaide Kuntz to Hudson Walker, October 31, 1945, McCausland files, AAA.

34. Kenneth Rexroth, *An Autobiographical Novel* (Garden City, N.Y.: Doubleday and Company, 1966), pp. 205–6.

In Hartley's Studio (pages 149–55)

1. See Hartley, "Somehow a Past," YCAL.

2. Chenoweth Hall, in conversation with author, July 1982.

3. Hartley to Kuntz, July 22, 1933, AAA.

4. Ibid., November 4, 1933, AAA.

5. Hartley, "Somehow a Past," YCAL.

6. Clair Spencer Evans's account is in Van Deren Coke, *The Painter and the Photograph from Delacroix to Warhol* (Albuquerque: University of New Mexico Press, 1972), pp. 212–13.

7. Ibid., p. 33 (for Lincoln); and the Brooklyn Museum object files (for Donne).

8. Hartley to Kuntz, February 2, 1940, AAA.

9. Ira Glackens, *William Glackens and the Ashcan Group* (New York: Crown Publishers, 1957), pp. 202–3.

10. Hartley to George, n.d., McCausland files (roll 272, frame 802), AAA.

CHRONOLOGY

1877 January 4—Edmund Hartley born in Lewiston, Maine, the last of eight children of Thomas and Eliza Jane Hartley.

1885 March 4—mother dies. Youngest sisters sent to Cleveland to live with older sister. Edmund lives with another older sister in Auburn, Maine, for eight years.

1889 Father marries Martha Marsden and moves to Cleveland.

1892 Edmund leaves school to work in Auburn shoe factory.

1893 Joins father and stepmother in Cleveland. Takes job as office boy in a marble quarry.

1896 Has weekly art lessons with John Semon, local painter in Cleveland.

1898 Summer—loses job in marble quarry. Takes outdoor painting class with Cullen Yates in Cleveland. Fall—enrolls in Cleveland School of Art on a scholarship. Teacher Nina Waldeck gives him a copy of Ralph Waldo Emerson's *Essays*.

1899 Spring—receives five-year annual stipend of $450 from Anne Walworth, a trustee of the Cleveland School of Art, to study art in New York. Fall—enters the New York School of Art (the Chase School); works with Luis Mora and Frank Vincent DuMond.

1900 Summer—returns to Lewiston, Maine, for the first visit in seven years; studies nature in countryside and executes flower and butterfly studies. Fall—leaves Chase School for the National Academy of Design, New York, and studies there for four years.

1901 Summer—joins art colony of Charles Fox and Curtis Perry in North Bridgton, Maine. Fall—returns to the National Academy.

1902 Spring—awarded Honorable Mention for composition and the Suydam Silver Medal for still-life drawing at the National Academy. Summer—lives in Center Lovell, Maine, near New Hampshire border; paints mountains. Fall—returns to the National Academy.

1903 Summer—returns to Center Lovell. Winter—attends the National Academy.

1904 Summer—paints in North Lovell. November—stipend from Anne Walworth runs out. Works as an extra with Proctor's Theater Company, New York.

1905 Summer—tours with Proctor's. Meets Horace Traubel and paints Walt Whitman's house in Camden, New Jersey.

1906 Summer—tours again with Proctor's. Fall—tour ends in Boston; Hartley returns to Lewiston, where he rents a studio on Lisbon Street and sends out announcements that he is available to give art lessons. Paints Impressionist landscapes through winter. Adopts stepmother's name, calling himself Edmund Marsden Hartley. Reads Maurice Maeterlinck, Edgar Allan Poe, Henrik Ibsen, and Irish poetry.

1907 Summer—gets a job erecting tents for Congress of Religions at Green Acre in Eliot, Maine. Fall—first solo exhibition held in home of Mrs. Ole Bull, adjacent to Green Acre complex. Returns to Lovell area to sketch for a month, then moves to Boston for winter.

148. Marsden Hartley, about age seven

149. Arnold Rönnebeck
Portrait Bust of Marsden Hartley,
1912
Bronze, no dimensions
Location unknown

"Nativeness is built of such primitive things, and whatever is one's nativeness, one holds and never loses no matter how far afield the traveling may be."

1908 Continues Impressionist landscapes. Spring—exhibits one painting at Rowlands Gallery, Boston, and meets Desmond Fitzgerald, a prominent collector, who buys a painting. Summer—returns to North Lovell and stays through winter.

1909 Continues painting through March, when he takes paintings to Boston and shows them to Maurice and Charles Prendergast; they write letters of introduction to William Glackens. Hartley goes to New York and shows work to some of The Eight at Glackens's studio. April—Seumas O'Sheel takes Hartley to 291 and introduces him to Alfred Stieglitz. May—Hartley's first major solo exhibition held at Stieglitz's gallery, 291. Meets N. E. Montross, who shows him paintings by Albert Pinkham Ryder. Summer—borrows space in the studio of his friend Ernest Roth, where he executes Dark Mountain paintings after Ryder. November—returns to Lewiston.

1910 Winter—returns to New York and joins the 291 circle of artists and writers associated with Stieglitz; sees Matisse and Rodin drawing shows at 291. Summer—goes back to North Lovell; paints Fauvist landscapes with high color and thick paint. December—returns to New York.

1911 Hospitalized for five weeks with scarlet fever. Spring—sees Picasso exhibition at 291 and experiments with Picasso-like abstractions; visits Baltimore and Philadelphia in unsuccessful attempt to sell paintings. June—returns to North Lovell and does series of Cézannesque still lifes of pears based on black-and-white reproductions. November—returns to New York and, with Arthur B. Davies, sees Cézanne works in Havemeyer collection.

1912 February—second solo exhibition held at 291. Through sale of a painting to Agnes Meyer, Stieglitz and Davies arrange for him to go to Europe. April 11—arrives in Paris and enters quickly into art life there. June—borrows Lee Simonson's studio at 18 rue Moulin de Beurre and paints still lifes in Matisse-Cézanne style; meets Gertrude and Leo Stein. July—introduced to German coterie, including Arnold Rönnebeck and his cousin Karl von Freyburg, and to Kandinsky's work in *The Blue Rider* and *On the Spiritual in Art*. Reads Christian mystics and William James's *Varieties of Religious Experience*. November—travels to London with his still-life paintings; meets Augustus John at Chenil Gallery; visits British Museum. Begins painting Intuitive Abstractions, including Musical Theme paintings.

1913 January—takes three-week trip to Berlin to visit Rönnebeck and his family; meets Kandinsky and Gabriele Münter on return trip through Munich; sees Franz Marc's work at Galerie Thannhauser. Spring—visits Stein's salon regularly; corresponds with Marc. April—Lee Simonson returns to Paris; Hartley leaves for Berlin and stays for several days at Sindelsdorf with Marc. Summer—paints prewar pageants and mystical paintings. Fall—exhibits five Intuitive Abstractions in Herbstsalon, Berlin, with Blue Rider artists. November 15—sails for New York with work for exhibition at 291.

1914 January—third solo show held at 291. February—spends ten days in Buffalo, New York, for show in home of Nina Bull. March—returns to Germany via London and Paris; paints emblematic color abstractions. Summer—paints Amerika series; continues painting after war is declared. October 7—Karl von Freyburg is killed; Hartley begins German Officer paintings in early November.

1915 Continues German Officer paintings in Berlin for nearly a year. October—exhibits forty-five paintings and some drawings at Münchener Graphik-Verlag, Berlin. December 11—returns to New York.

1916 Lives in New York. Pays short visit to Mabel Dodge in Croton-on-Hudson and attends Dodge's salon in Greenwich Village. Does cubistic portraits and still lifes. April—fourth solo exhibition held at 291; German Officer pictures meet with disfavor. Summer—guest of John Reed at Provincetown, Massachusetts, with Carl Sprinchorn, Charles Demuth, William and Marguerite Zorach, and others. Fall—stays in Provincetown, then returns to New York. December—goes to Bermuda with Demuth. First essays published in *New Republic* and *Seven Arts*.

1917 Tires of Bermuda landscape and does still-life-through-window pictures. May—returns to New York. Summer—visits Lewiston and then joins Hamilton Easter Field's art colony in Ogunquit, Maine. Does paintings on glass. Fall—returns to New York and lives in an apartment owned by Field in Brooklyn Heights.

1918 June—at the suggestion of Mabel Dodge and others travels to New Mexico; stays in Taos through summer, where he does still lifes and pastel landscapes. November—dislikes Taos and, concerned about influenza epidemic, moves to Santa Fe. Writes essays on Indians and American landscape. First poems published in *Poetry*.

1919 February—visits Carl Sprinchorn in La Cañada, California; meets Robert McAlmon at poetry reading. Visits San Francisco. Summer—returns to Santa Fe, where he does second series of pastels and some oils of New Mexico landscape. Santa Fe Museum buys one of his paintings. November—returns to New York with a stop in Chicago, where he sees Sherwood Anderson and Harriet Monroe.

1920 Works on New Mexico paintings. Spring—becomes involved with New York Dada movement and the Société Anonyme, founded by Marcel Duchamp and Katherine Dreier. Summer—stays in Gloucester, Massachusetts. Oc-tober—returns to New York. Introduces McAlmon to William Carlos Williams and works on first issue of *Contact* with them. Continues to publish poems in *Poetry* and *Little Review.*

1921 Continues involvement with Société Anonyme. *Adventures in the Arts* published by Boni, Liveright. May 17—auction of 117 works at Anderson Galleries, arranged by Stieglitz and Mitchell Kennerly, brings enough money to finance another trip to Europe. Summer—arrives in Paris; visits sculptor John Storrs in Orléans. November—moves to Berlin, where he lives well because of the inflated exchange rate.

1922 Paints still lifes of fruit, bowls, baskets, and bread. Fall—does lithographs of similar still-life arrangements. *Twenty-five Poems* published by McAlmon in Paris.

1923 Spring—begins series of New Mexico Recollections. Summer—does series of pastel studies of male and female nudes. Fall—travels to Vienna and Italy and stays in Florence for eight weeks; also visits Arezzo, Rome, and Naples. Writes essays about art encountered on travels.

1924 Winter—sails for New York. February—arranges with a syndicate of five businessmen for a yearly stipend of two thousand dollars in exchange for paintings; this enables him to continue living in Europe for the next four years. Summer—returns to Paris via London, Brussels, Antwerp. Uses George Biddle's studio, where he continues New Mexico Recollections and does series of fish still lifes and recollections of Maine.

1925 August—moves to Vence, France, for a year and does landscapes of Italian Alps around Gattière and Carros. Writes *Provençal Preludes* and *Bach for Breakfast* poems.

1926 March—visits Paris and sees Cézanne exhibition at Bernheim-Jeune galleries, which rekindles his interest in Cézanne. October—moves to Aix-en-

150. Arnold Rönnebeck
Portrait Mask of Marsden Hartley,
1912
Bronze, life-size
Location unknown

"Artists and religionists are never very far apart, they go to the sources of revelation for what they choose to experience and what they report is the degree of their experiences. Intellect wishes to arrange—intuition wishes to accept."

151. Marsden Hartley at Les Baux, France, 1929

"I see the possibility of being 'made new' again and the gift of rebirth is all that lets anyone really live.... The great secret ... is never to get stuck, imprisoned in common social patterns. They always paralyze the real quality of life—the 'going onward' is all that matters, and the dead moments in one's life through trying to be a unit in any society or social concept are terrifying really."

Provence. Lives in Maison Maria, in the Château Noir forest, and works in Cézannesque manner.

1927 Winter—travels to Paris, Berlin, and Hamburg, returning to Aix in summer. Does Mont Sainte-Victoire paintings and pencil and silverpoint drawings of trees and rocks. December—goes to Paris.

1928 January—travels to America. Stays in New York and then visits Chicago for his exhibition at Arts Club of Chicago. Visits Arnold Rönnebeck in Denver, where Hartley lectures on Cézanne. Summer—visits friends in Conway, New Hampshire, and spends two weeks in Georgetown, Maine, with Gaston and Isabel Lachaise and Paul and Rebecca Strand. August—sails again for France. Winter—stays in Paris in large apartment and does seashell still lifes.

1929 April—returns to Maison Maria in Aix-en-Provence, depressed over critical reaction to his painting and to his long absence from home. Reads George Santayana, Miguel Unamuno, and Christian mystics. November—travels to Marseilles, where he meets Hart Crane by chance; then goes on alone to Toulouse, Albi, Paris, and London for Christmas. Proceeds to Hamburg, Berlin, and Dresden.

1930 March—sails for New York, where he lives in Brooklyn Heights. Rebecca Strand types his book of essays about Europe, "Varied Patterns." June—goes to Sugar Hill, near Franconia, New Hampshire, for summer with a Polish friend who has a car and drives him to painting sites. Visits Montreal and Quebec and returns for fall colors in New Hampshire. November—returns to Brooklyn and lives at Pierrepont Hotel.

1931 Winter—ill and very depressed. Cared for by Adelaide Kuntz and other friends. Spring—receives a Guggenheim fellowship and decides to go to Mexico. July—returns to Gloucester to paint

Dogtown Common; stays through mid-December. Visits family in Cleveland for Christmas.

1932 March—takes a ship to Vera Cruz and then goes to Mexico City. April—Hart Crane commits suicide on his way back to the United States after being in Mexico on a Guggenheim fellowship. May—Hartley moves to Cuernavaca because of his health problems caused by the altitude in Mexico City. Has studio with a view of Popocatépetl and paints several versions of the volcano. Has access to library of occult literature. Executes Mexico mystical-fantasy pictures. November—moves back to Mexico City.

1933 February—exhibition held at Galeria de la Escuela Central de Artes Plasticas, Mexico City. March—denied renewal for second year of Guggenheim fellowship. April—sails for Hamburg, where he stays for the summer. September—determines to paint Alps and goes to Garmisch-Partenkirchen. Walks great distances in vicinity and does many drawings. Winter—executes paintings and lithographs from studies. Travels to Munich. Reads Shakespeare and Gertrude Stein's *Autobiography of Alice B. Toklas* and starts his own autobiography.

1934 February—returns to New York and works on easel program of the Public Works of Art Project; rebels against constraints and quits after one month. July—returns to Gloucester and does second series of Dogtown works. Fall—returns to New York.

1935 January 4—destroys one hundred paintings and drawings in storage because he cannot afford to pay storage bill. Very ill and depressed. Summer—travels to Bermuda to recuperate. Executes flower and fish "fancies." September—sails for Lunenberg, Nova Scotia. Boards with Francis Mason family on Eastern Points island. December—returns to New York.

1936 Applies for an assignment with the Works Progress Administration (WPA). March—exhibition at An American Place received well. April—gives lecture entitled "And the Nude Has Descended the Staircase" at the Museum of Modern Art in connection with a Surrealist exhibition. Continues publishing essays in various periodicals. July—returns to Eastern Points to live with Masons; does third Dogtown series from memory. September—Alty and Donny Mason killed in a hurricane. December—Hartley returns to New York.

1937 April—last exhibition with Stieglitz held at An American Place. Hudson Walker takes nine paintings from exhibition for his own gallery. June—Hartley visits family in Auburn, Maine. Rents house in Georgetown near Gaston Lachaise's home; stays for five months and talks of becoming "the" painter of Maine. December—moves for winter to Portland, Maine.

1938 February—goes to New York for first solo exhibition at Hudson Walker Gallery. Summer—resides on Vinalhaven, an island off Rockland, Maine. Works on seascapes and "archaic" portraits of Nova Scotia people and Ryder. November—spends a week visiting in Lewiston and Auburn, then moves to Boston for the winter.

1939 February—goes to New York for second solo exhibition at Walker Gallery. June—returns to Maine—to Portland, Lewiston, Auburn, and then Bagaduce Farm in West Brookville as guest of Clair Spencer and John Evans. Waldo Pierce takes him to Corea, Maine, where Hartley decides to live the next season. September—moves to Bangor for winter and teaches art classes. October—takes eight-day trip to Mt. Katahdin. Winter—works on Katahdin pictures in Bangor. December—exhibition at Symphony Hall, Boston, is well received.

1940 March—visits New York for third solo exhibition at Walker Gallery. Summer—boards with Forest and Katie Young, a lobster fisherman and his wife, in Corea. Hartley works on figure and religious paintings. Wins J. Henry Scheidt Memorial Prize at Pennsylvania Academy of the Fine Arts. Publishes *Androscoggin,* a collection of poems, with Leon Tebbetts, a Maine publisher.

1941 January—moves to Bangor for several months. March—goes to New York and lives in Winslow Hotel. July—returns to Maine and visits Portland and Old Orchard Beach, where he does studies of figures on beach, and then moves back to Corea. Concentrates on writing and revises his autobiography ("Somehow a Past"), "Cleophas and His Own" (about his Nova Scotia experience), and "The Spangle of Existence" (another collection of essays). Publishes second volume of poetry, *Sea Burial,* with Leon Tebbetts. Winter—travels to Cincinnati for joint exhibition with Stuart Davis at Cincinnati Art Museum, then to Cleveland for Christmas with family.

1942 Gives lecture at Cincinnati Art Museum, "Is Art Necessary?" March—exhibition held at Macbeth Gallery, New York. Summer—returns to Corea. Paul Rosenberg becomes his dealer. Winter—*Lobster Fishermen at Corea* wins Fourth Painting Purchase Prize ($2000) at Metropolitan Museum of Art's *Artists for Victory* exhibition.

1943 January—returns to New York. Writes last series of poems, "Patterns for Prayers." Summer—returns to Corea. Is very ill most of the summer. September 2—dies of heart failure in hospital at Ellsworth, Maine.

152. Marsden Hartley at Dogtown Common, Cape Ann, Massachusetts, 1934

"I don't want escape via intellectual ruses—I want affirmations via passionate embraces, & you can't have life unless you live it."

EXHIBITIONS

Solo Exhibitions

1907 Exhibition in the home of Mrs. Ole Bull, Eliot, Maine, late summer.

1909 *Exhibition of Paintings in Oil by Mr. Marsden Hartley of Maine,* Photo-Secession Galleries ("291"), New York, May 8–18.

1912 *Recent Paintings and Drawings by Marsden Hartley,* Photo-Secession Galleries, New York, February 7–26.

1914 *Paintings by Marsden Hartley,* Photo-Secession Galleries, New York, January 12–February 14.
Exhibition in the home of Nina Bull, Buffalo, New York, February.
Exhibition in the home of Florence Bradley, Chicago, early March.

1915 *Paintings by Marsden Hartley: "The Mountain Series,"* Daniel Gallery, New York, January–February 9.
Schames Galerie, Frankfurt, September.
Münchener Graphik-Verlag, Berlin, October.

1916 *Paintings by Marsden Hartley,* Photo-Secession Galleries, New York, April 4–May 22.

1917 *Marsden Hartley's Recent Work,* Photo-Secession Galleries, New York, January 22–February 7.
Ogunquit School of Painting and Sculpture, Ogunquit, Maine, late August–September.

1920 *Recent Paintings and Drawings by Marsden Hartley,* Daniel Gallery, New York, January 2–21.

1928 *Paintings and Water Colors by Marsden Hartley,* Arts Club of Chicago, February 28–March 13.

1929 *Hartley Exhibition,* Intimate Gallery, New York, January.

1930 *Marsden Hartley—New Paintings,* An American Place, New York, December 15–January 18.

1932 *Pictures of New England by a New Englander: Recent Paintings of Dogtown, Cape Ann, Massachusetts,* Downtown Gallery, New York, April 26–May 15.

1933 *Exposicion Marsden Hartley,* Galeria de la Escuela Central de Artes Plasticas, Mexico City, February 28–March 7.

1936 *Marsden Hartley,* An American Place, New York, March 22–April 14.

1937 *Marsden Hartley: Exhibition of Recent Paintings,* An American Place, New York, April 20–May 17.

1938 *Marsden Hartley: Recent Paintings of Maine,* Hudson Walker Gallery, New York, February 28–April 2.

1939 *Marsden Hartley: 25th One-Man Show,* Hudson Walker Gallery, New York, March 6–April 8.
Marsden Hartley, Symphony Hall, Boston, December–January 6.

1940 *Marsden Hartley: Recent Paintings of Maine,* Hudson Walker Gallery, New York, March 11–30.

1942 *Marsden Hartley,* Macbeth Gallery, New York, March 9–28.
Early Drawings by Marsden Hartley,

153. *Floral Life: Debonaire,* 1920
Oil on canvas, 22 × 16 in.
University Art Museum, University of Minnesota, Minneapolis; Bequest of Hudson Walker from the Ione and Hudson Walker Collection

M. Knoedler and Company, New York, October 12–31.

1943 *Recent Works by Marsden Hartley*, Paul Rosenberg and Company, New York, February 2–27 [misdated 1942].

Marsden Hartley, Phillips Memorial Gallery, Washington, D.C., October 24–November 23.

1944 *Marsden Hartley Memorial Exhibition*, Columbus Gallery of Fine Arts, Columbus, Ohio, January 8–February 7.

Marsden Hartley, Museum of Modern Art, New York, October 24–January 14. There was a catalog that also documented a simultaneous solo exhibition for Lyonel Feininger.

Drawings and Paintings by Marsden Hartley, M. Knoedler and Company and Paul Rosenberg and Company, New York, December 11–30. Drawings were shown at Knoedler, paintings at Rosenberg, with a joint catalog.

1945 *Marsden Hartley: Paintings and Drawings*, November 26–December 15.

Marsden Hartley: Memorial Exhibition, December 7–31.

1946 *Marsden Hartley Drawings*, Columbus Gallery of Fine Arts, Columbus, Ohio, April 8–30.

Marsden Hartley, Los Angeles County Museum, May 12–June 13.

1948 *Exhibition of Paintings by Marsden Hartley before 1932*, Bertha Schaefer Gallery, New York, April 5–17.

Paintings by Marsden Hartley, Paul Rosenberg and Company, New York, October 18–November 12.

1950 *Paintings by Marsden Hartley*, Paul Rosenberg and Company, New York, January 9–28.

1951 *Paintings by Marsden Hartley*, Paul Rosenberg and Company, New York, April 16–May 12.

Marsden Hartley Retrospective, University Art Museum, University of Minnesota, Minneapolis, May 5–June 13. Selected works toured the United States, July 20, 1952–June 28, 1954.

1955 *The Berlin Period, 1913–1915*, Martha Jackson Gallery, New York, January 3–29.

Paintings by Marsden Hartley, Paul Rosenberg and Company, New York, April 4–30.

1957 *Marsden Hartley*, Babcock Galleries, New York, April 2–May 4.

Hartley: Landscape and Still Life in Oil, Martha Jackson Gallery, New York, May 14–June 14.

1958 *Marsden Hartley*, Museum of New Mexico Art Gallery, Santa Fe, February.

1959 *Marsden Hartley*, Babcock Galleries, New York, December 8–January 3.

Marsden Hartley: Drawings and Lithographs, Babcock Galleries, New York, January 5–24.

1960 *Hartley, 1877–1943*, Babcock Galleries, New York, January 4–30.

Drawings by Marsden Hartley, Paul Rosenberg and Company, New York, February 16–March 12.

Marsden Hartley, Alfredo Valente Gallery, New York, September 28–November 5.

Marsden Hartley, American Federation of Arts Traveling Exhibition: Marion Koogler McNay Art Institute, San Antonio, Texas, December 6–31; Stedelijk Museum, Amsterdam, February 3–March 6, 1961; Amerika Haus, Berlin, March 15–April 6; Stadt und Lenbachgalerie, Munich, April 16–May 7; American Embassy, London, June 15–July 15; Portland Museum of Art, Portland, Maine, August 12–September 2; Walker Art Center, Minneapolis, September 25–October 31; City Art Museum, Saint Louis, November 15–December 15; Cincinnati Art Museum, January 1–31, 1962; Whitney Museum of American Art, New York, March 7–April 8.

1961 *Marsden Hartley: Drawings and Pastels*, Babcock Galleries, New York, April 18–May 6.

Marsden Hartley: Paintings and

Drawings, David Anderson Gallery, New York, April 22–May 20.

1962 *Marsden Hartley,* Alfredo Valente Gallery, New York, March 5–30.

Marsden Hartley, 1877–1943, Shore Galleries, Boston, March 7–24.

Marsden Hartley, Babcock Galleries, New York, March 27–April 14.

1964 *Marsden Hartley: Oils, Drawings, Pastels, 1909–1964 [sic],* Alfredo Valente Gallery, New York, March 24–April 30.

1966 *Late Works of Marsden Hartley,* American Federation of Arts Traveling Exhibition: Birmingham Museum of Art, Birmingham, Alabama, October 2–23; University Art Museum, University of Minnesota, Minneapolis, November 6–27; Oklahoma Art Center, Oklahoma City, January 15–February 5, 1967; Portland Art Museum, Portland, Oregon, February 19–March 12; University of Iowa Art Museum, Iowa City, March 26–April 16; Colby College, Waterville, Maine, May 14–June 11; Charles and Emma Freye Art Museum, Seattle, July 29–August 20; Wichita Art Museum, Wichita, Kansas, September 6–27; Munson-Williams-Proctor Institute, Utica, New York, October 11–November 1.

1967 *Still Life Compositions: Lithographs, 1923–24,* Martha Jackson Gallery, New York, October 28–November 18.

1968 *Marsden Hartley: A Selection of Paintings and Drawings of the Twenties and Thirties,* M. Knoedler and Company, New York, January 9–27.

Marsden Hartley: Painter/Poet, 1877–1943, University Galleries, University of Southern California, Los Angeles, November 20–December 20; Tucson Art Center, Tucson, Arizona, January 10–February 16, 1969; University Art Museum, University of Texas at Austin, March 10–April 27.

1969 *Marsden Hartley: A Retrospective Exhibition,* Bernard Danenberg Galleries, New York, September 16–October 4.

1970 *Ninety-nine Drawings by Marsden Hartley,* Smithsonian Institution Traveling Exhibition, toured the United States, November 2, 1970–February 24, 1974.

1972 *Marsden Hartley,* Babcock Galleries, New York, January 8–29.

Marsden Hartley: Lithographs and Related Works, University of Kansas Museum of Art, Lawrence, March 19–April 16.

1974 *Marsden Hartley,* Pierce Gallery, Bangor, Maine, August 16–September 14.

1975 *Marsden Hartley,* Babcock Galleries, New York, October 1–29.

1977 *Marsden Hartley, 1877–1943.* C. W. Post Art Gallery, Greenvale, New York, November 6–December 14.

1978 *Marsden Hartley Memorial Collection,* Treat Gallery, Bates College, Lewiston, Maine, May 14–June 30.

1980 *Marsden Hartley, 1877–1943.* Babcock Galleries, New York, March.

Marsden Hartley, Whitney Museum of American Art, New York, March 4–May 25; Art Institute of Chicago, June 10–August 3; Amon Carter Museum of Western Art, Fort Worth, September 5–October 26; University Art Museum, University of California, Berkeley, November 12–January 4, 1981.

Marsden Hartley in New England, Barridoff Galleries, Portland, Maine, July 12–September 3.

1982 *Marsden Hartley: Visionary of Maine,* University of Maine at Presque Isle, September 19–October 21; Joan Whitney Payson Gallery, Westbrook, Maine, October 31–December 2; Treat Gallery, Bates College, Lewiston, Maine, December 16–February 17, 1983; Brick Store Museum, Kennebunk, Maine, February 27–March 30; Colby College Museum of Art, Waterville, Maine, April 10–May 15.

1984 *Marsden Hartley, 1908–1942: The Ione and Hudson D. Walker Collection,* University Art Museum, University of Minnesota, Minneapolis, circulated by the Art Museum Association of America throughout the United States, January 20, 1984–June 6, 1986.

1985 *Marsden Hartley: Paintings and Drawings,* Salander-O'Reilly Galleries, New York, March 6–April 27.

Marsden Hartley: Soliloquy in Dogtown, Cape Ann Historical Association, Gloucester, Massachusetts, July 26–September 21.

1986 *Marsden Hartley Pastels: The Ione and Hudson Walker Collection,* University Art Museum, University of Minnesota, Minneapolis, March 31–June 1, 1986.

1987 *Marsden Hartley and Nova Scotia,* Mount Saint Vincent University Art Gallery, Halifax, Nova Scotia, October 22–November 23; Art Gallery of Ontario, Toronto, January 6–March 13, 1988.

1988 *Marsden Hartley: Paintings and Drawings,* Salander-O'Reilly Galleries, New York, January 8–February 27.

Marsden Hartley: The Last Decade, Vanderwoude Tananbaum, New York, January 13–February 27.

Group Exhibitions

1910 *Younger American Painters,* Photo-Secession Galleries, New York, March 21–April 15.

1911 *An Independent Exhibition,* Gallery of the Society of Beaux-Arts Architects, New York, March 26–April 21.

1913 *International Exhibition of Modern Art,* 69th Infantry Regiment Armory, New York, February 17–March 15; Art Institute of Chicago, March 24–April 15; Copley Hall, Copley Society of Boston, April 28–May 18.

Erster deutscher Herbstsalon, Der Sturm, Berlin, September 20–December 1.

1916 *The Forum Exhibition of Modern American Painters,* Anderson Galleries, New York, March 13–25.

1917 *First Annual Exhibition of the Society of Independent Artists,* Grand Central Palace, New York, April 10–May 6.

1921 *Fifth Annual Exhibition of the Society of Independent Artists,* Waldorf-Astoria, New York, February 26–March 24.

Seventy-five Pictures by James N. Rosenberg and 117 Pictures by Marsden Hartley, Anderson Galleries, New York, May 10–17 (an auction was held May 17).

1925 *Six American Painters and Two American Sculptors,* Galerie Briant-Robert, Paris, January 19–February 19.

1930 *Painting and Sculpture by Living Americans,* Museum of Modern Art, New York, December 2–January 20, 1931.

1932 *First Biennial Exhibition of Contemporary American Painting,* Whitney Museum of American Art, New York, November 22–January 5, 1933. (Hartley was also included in the Whitney Annual Exhibitions for 1934, 1937, 1938, 1940, 1940–41, 1942–43.)

1935 *Abstract Painting in America,* Whitney Museum of American Art, New York, February 12–March 22.

1936 *New Horizons in American Art,* Museum of Modern Art, New York, September 14–October 12.

1940 *The One Hundred and Thirty-Fifth Annual Exhibition of Painting and Sculpture,* Pennsylvania Academy of the Fine Arts, Philadelphia, January 28–March 3.

1941 *Contemporary Painting in the United States,* Metropolitan Museum of Art, New York, April 19–27.

Marsden Hartley/Stuart Davis, Cincinnati Art Museum, October 24–November 24.

1942 *Artists for Victory,* Metropolitan Museum of Art, New York, December 7–February 22, 1943. Hartley received Fourth Painting Prize of $2,000 for *Lobster Fishermen.*

1943 *Painting in the United States,* Carnegie Institute, Pittsburgh, October 14–December 12.

1946 *Museums' Choice Exhibition,* Museum of Art, Rhode Island School of Design, Providence, February 6–28.

Five Expressionists, Allen Memorial Art Museum, Oberlin College, Oberlin, Ohio, April.

Pioneers of Modern Art in America, Whitney Museum of American Art, New York, April 9–May 19.

1949 *American Painting in Our Century,* Institute of Contemporary Art, Boston, February.

1951 *Abstract Painting and Sculpture in America,* Museum of Modern Art, New York, January 23–March 25.

1958 *Stieglitz Circle,* Pomona College Galleries, Claremont, California, October 11–November 15.

1963 *Taos and Santa Fe: The Artist's Environment, 1882–1942,* Amon Carter Museum of Western Art, Fort Worth, April 5–May 26.

1964 *Marsden Hartley/John Marin,* La Jolla Museum of Art, La Jolla, California, February 12–March 27.

1965 *Roots of Abstract Art in America, 1910–1930,* National Collection of Fine Arts, Smithsonian Institution, Washington, D.C., December 2–January 6.

1975 *Avant-Garde Painting and Sculpture in America, 1910–25,* Delaware Art Museum, Wilmington, April 4–May 18.

1977 *The Modern Spirit: American Paintings, 1908–1935,* Royal Scottish Academy, Edinburgh, August 20–September 11; Hayward Gallery, London, September 28–November 20.

1978 *Synchromism and American Color Abstraction, 1910–1925,* Whitney Museum of American Art, New York, January 24–March 26; exhibition traveled in the United States through March 24, 1979.

1979 *2 Jahrzehnte amerikanische Malerei, 1920–1940,* Städtische Kunsthalle Düsseldorf, June 10–August 12.

1984 *The Mystic North: Symbolist Landscape Painting in Northern Europe and North America, 1890–1940,* Art Gallery of Ontario, Toronto, January 13–March 11; Cincinnati Art Museum, March 31–May 13.

1986 *The Advent of Modernism: Post-Impressionism and North American Art, 1900–1918,* High Museum of Art, Atlanta, March 4–May 11; Center for the Fine Arts, Miami, June 22–August 31; Brooklyn Museum, New York, November 26–January 19, 1987; Glenbow Museum, Calgary, Alberta, February 21–April 19.

Art in New Mexico, 1900–1945: Paths to Taos and Santa Fe, National Museum of American Art, Smithsonian Institution, Washington, D.C., March 7–June 15; Cincinnati Art Museum, July 18–September 21; Museum of Fine Arts, Houston, October 31–January 4, 1987; Denver Art Museum, February 18–April 19.

The Spiritual in Art: Abstract Painting 1890–1985, Los Angeles County Museum of Art, November 23, 1986–March 8, 1987; Museum of Contemporary Art, Chicago, April 17–July 19; Haags Gemeentemuseum, The Hague, September 1–November 22.

1987 *The Expressionist Landscape,* Birmingham Museum of Art, Birmingham, Alabama, September 11–November 4; IBM Gallery of Science and Art, New York, November 27–January 30, 1988.

PUBLIC COLLECTIONS

Amsterdam, Netherlands, Stedelijk Museum

Andover, Massachusetts, Addison Gallery of American Art, Phillips Academy

Ann Arbor, Michigan, University of Michigan Museum of Art

Athens, Georgia, University of Georgia, Georgia Museum of Art

Atlanta, Georgia, High Museum of Art

Austin, Texas, University of Texas, Archer M. Huntington Art Gallery

Austin, Texas, University of Texas, Humanities Research Center

Baltimore, Maryland, Baltimore Museum of Art

Berkeley, California, University of California, University Art Museum

Bethlehem, Pennsylvania, Lehigh University Art Galleries

Bloomington, Indiana, Indiana University Art Museum

Boston, Massachusetts, Museum of Fine Arts

Boulder, Colorado, University of Colorado Museum

Brooklyn, New York, Brooklyn Museum

Brunswick, Maine, Bowdoin College Museum of Art

Buffalo, New York, Albright-Knox Art Gallery

Cambridge, Massachusetts, Harvard University, Fogg Art Museum

Chattanooga, Tennessee, Hunter Museum of Art

Chicago, Illinois, Art Institute of Chicago

Chicago, Illinois, Terra Museum of American Art

Cleveland, Ohio, Cleveland Museum of Art

Clinton, New York, Hamilton College Art Gallery

Colorado Springs, Colorado, Colorado Springs Fine Arts Center

Columbus, Ohio, Columbus Museum of Art

Dayton, Ohio, Dayton Art Institute

Denver, Colorado, Denver Art Museum

Des Moines, Iowa, Des Moines Art Center

Detroit, Michigan, Detroit Institute of Arts

Fort Worth, Texas, Amon Carter Museum

Hartford, Connecticut, Wadsworth Atheneum

Huntington, New York, Heckscher Museum

Indianapolis, Indiana, Purdue University at Indianapolis, Herron Gallery

Iowa City, Iowa, University of Iowa Museum of Art

Ithaca, New York, Cornell University, Andrew Dickson White Museum of Art

Kansas City, Missouri, Nelson-Atkins Museum of Art

Lewiston, Maine, Bates College, Olin Art Center

Lewiston, Maine, Lewiston Public Library

Lincoln, Nebraska, University of Nebraska, Sheldon Memorial Art Gallery

Los Angeles, California, Los Angeles County Museum of Art

Louisville, Kentucky, J. B. Speed Art Museum

Manchester, New Hampshire, Currier Gallery of Art

Merion, Pennsylvania, Barnes Foundation Museum of Art

Milwaukee, Wisconsin, Milwaukee Art Museum

Minneapolis, Minnesota, Minneapolis Institute of Arts

154. *Maine Coast Still Life,* 1940
Oil on Masonite, 40 × 30 in.
Walker Art Center, Minneapolis;
Gift of Mrs. Archie D. Walker,
Josiah Bell Hudson Memorial,
1946

Minneapolis, Minnesota, University of Minnesota, University Art Museum

Minneapolis, Minnesota, Walker Art Center

Nashville, Tennessee, Fisk University, Carl Van Vechten Gallery of Fine Arts

Newark, New Jersey, Newark Museum

New Britain, Connecticut, New Britain Museum of American Art

New Haven, Connecticut, Yale University, Collection of American Literature, Beinecke Rare Book and Manuscript Library

New Haven, Connecticut, Yale University Art Gallery

New Orleans, Louisiana, New Orleans Museum of Art

New York, New York, Metropolitan Museum of Art

New York, New York, Museum of Modern Art

New York, New York, New York University Art Collection, Grey Art Gallery and Study Center

New York, New York, Whitney Museum of American Art

Northampton, Massachusetts, Smith College Museum of Art

Ogunquit, Maine, Museum of Art of Ogunquit

Omaha, Nebraska, Joslyn Art Museum

Orono, Maine, University of Maine Art Galleries

Philadelphia, Pennsylvania, Philadelphia Museum of Art

Phoenix, Arizona, Phoenix Art Museum

Pittsburgh, Pennsylvania, Carnegie Museum of Art

Pittsfield, Massachusetts, Berkshire Museum

Portland, Maine, Portland Museum of Art

Portland, Oregon, Portland Art Museum

Poughkeepsie, New York, Vassar College Art Gallery

Raleigh, North Carolina, North Carolina Museum of Art

Richmond, Virginia, Virginia Museum of Fine Arts

Roswell, New Mexico, Roswell Museum and Art Center

Saint Louis, Missouri, Saint Louis Art Museum

Saint Louis, Missouri, Washington University Gallery of Art

San Antonio, Texas, Marion Koogler McNay Art Museum

San Antonio, Texas, Witte Memorial Museum

San Diego, California, Fine Arts Gallery of San Diego

San Francisco, California, Fine Arts Museums of San Francisco

San Francisco, California, San Francisco Museum of Modern Art

Santa Barbara, California, Santa Barbara Museum of Art

Santa Fe, New Mexico, Museum of New Mexico

Sarasota, Florida, John and Mable Ringling Museum of Art

Seattle, Washington, Charles and Emma Frye Art Museum

Seattle, Washington, Seattle Art Museum

Seattle, Washington, University of Washington, Henry Art Gallery

Syracuse, New York, Everson Museum of Art

Toledo, Ohio, Toledo Museum of Art

Tucson, Arizona, Tucson Museum of Art

Utica, New York, Munson-Williams-Proctor Institute

Waltham, Massachusetts, Brandeis University, Rose Art Museum

Washington, D.C., Corcoran Gallery of Art

Washington, D.C., Hirshhorn Museum and Sculpture Garden, Smithsonian Institution

Washington, D.C., National Gallery of Art

Washington, D.C., National Museum of American Art

Washington, D.C., Phillips Collection

Waterville, Maine, Colby College Museum of Art

Wichita, Kansas, Wichita Art Museum

Williamstown, Massachusetts, Williams College Museum of Art

Wilmington, Delaware, Delaware Art Museum

Worcester, Massachusetts, Worcester Art Museum

Youngstown, Ohio, Butler Institute of American Art

SELECTED BIBLIOGRAPHY

Books by Hartley

For a complete list of Hartley's individually published poems, statements, and articles, see *On Art,* edited by Gail R. Scott, 1982.

Adventures in the Arts: Informal Chapters on Painters, Vaudeville and Poets. New York: Boni, Liveright, 1921; reprinted New York: Hacker Books, 1972.

Androscoggin [poetry]. Portland, Maine: Falmouth Publishing House, 1940.

Cleophas and His Own: A North Atlantic Tragedy, facsimile edition. Halifax: Nova Scotia College of Art and Design, 1982.

The Collected Poems of Marsden Hartley, 1904–1943. Edited and with an introduction by Gail R. Scott and a foreword by Robert Creeley. Santa Rosa, Calif.: Black Sparrow Press, 1987.

Eight Poems and One Essay. Lewiston, Maine: Bates College, 1976.

Heart's Gate: Letters between Marsden Hartley and Horace Traubel, 1906–1915. Edited and with an introduction by William Innes Homer. High-lands, N.C.: Jargon Society, 1982.

On Art. Edited and with an introduction by Gail R. Scott. New York: Horizon Press, 1982.

Sea Burial [poetry]. Portland, Maine: Leon Tebbetts Editions, 1941.

Selected Poems. Edited by Henry W. Wells. New York: Viking Press, 1945.

Twenty-five Poems. Paris: Contact Publishing Company, 1923.

Monographs and Solo-Exhibition Catalogs

Eldredge, Charles. *Marsden Hartley: Lithographs and Related Works,* exhibition catalog. Lawrence: University of Kansas Museum of Art, 1972.

Ferguson, Gerald, ed. *Marsden Hartley and Nova Scotia.* Halifax, Nova Scotia: Mount Saint Vincent University Art Gallery, 1987. Includes Ronald Paulson, "Marsden Hartley's Search for the Father(land)," and Gail R. Scott, "Cleophas and His Own: The Making of a Narrative."

Gambone, Robert. *Marsden Hartley Pastels: The Ione and Hudson Walker Collection,* exhibition catalog. Minneapolis: University of Minnesota Art Museum, 1986.

Haskell, Barbara. *Marsden Hartley,* exhibition catalog. New York: Whitney Museum of American Art and New York University Press, 1980.

McCausland, Elizabeth. *Marsden Hart-ley.* Minneapolis: University of Minnesota Press, 1952.

——. *Marsden Hartley,* exhibition catalog. Amsterdam: Stedelijk Museum, 1961.

Marsden Hartley, 1877–1943, exhibition catalog. Greenvale, N.Y.: C. W. Post Art Gallery, 1977.

Marsden Hartley, 1877–1943, exhibition catalog. New York: Babcock Galleries, 1980.

Marsden Hartley in New England, exhibition catalog. Portland, Maine: Barridoff Galleries, 1980.

Marsden Hartley, 1908–1942: The Ione and Hudson D. Walker Collection, exhibition catalog. Minneapolis: University Art Museum, University of Minnesota, 1984.

Marsden Hartley: Painter/Poet, 1877–1943, exhibition catalog. Los Angeles: University Galleries, University of Southern California, 1968.

Marsden Hartley: Paintings and Drawings, exhibition catalog. New York: Salander-O'Reilly Galleries, 1985.

Marsden Hartley: Paintings and Drawings, exhibition catalog. New York: Salander-O'Reilly Galleries, 1988.

Marsden Hartley: Soliloquy in Dogtown, exhibition catalog. Gloucester, Mass.: Cape Ann Historical Association, 1985.

Mitchell, William J. *Ninety-nine Drawings by Marsden Hartley*, exhibition catalog. Lewiston, Maine: Bates College Art Department, 1970.

Scott, Gail R. *Marsden Hartley: Visionary of Maine*, exhibition brochure. Presque Isle: University of Maine at Presque Isle, 1982.

Books, Articles, and Group-Exhibition Catalogs

The Advent of Modernism: Post-Impressionism and North American Art, 1900–1918, exhibition catalog. Atlanta: High Museum of Art, 1986. Includes essays by Peter Morrin, Judith Zilczer, and William C. Agee, with catalog notes on Hartley by Gail Levin.

American Paintings in the Ferdinand Howald Collection. Columbus, Ohio: Columbus Gallery of Fine Arts, 1969. Catalog of works owned by Ferdinand Howald, one of Hartley's early patrons, with introduction by Edgar P. Richardson and catalog by Marcia Tucker.

Art in New Mexico, 1900–1945: Paths to Taos and Santa Fe, exhibition catalog. Washington, D.C.: National Museum of American Art, Smithsonian Institution; New York: Abbeville Press, 1986.

Barnett, Vivian Endicott. "Marsden Hartley's Return to Maine." *Arts Magazine* 54 (October 1979): 172–76.

Barry, Roxana. "The Age of Blood and Iron: Marsden Hartley in Berlin." *Arts Magazine* 54 (October 1979): 166–71.

Breuning, Margaret. "The Hard Core of Hartley's Native Genius." *Art Digest* 24 (January 15, 1950): 45.

————. "Marsden Hartley Seen in Late, Great Works." *Art Digest* 23 (November 1, 1948): 12.

Broder, Patricia. "Marsden Hartley: In Search of American Icons." In *The American West: The Modern Vision*. Boston: Little, Brown and Company; A New York Graphic Society Book, 1984, pp. 129–49.

Burlingame, Robert. "Marsden Hartley: A Study of His Life and Creative Achievement." Ph.D. dissertation, Brown University, 1953.

Coates, Robert M. "Marsden Hartley's Maine." *New Yorker* 24 (October 30, 1948): 85.

————. "Sea and Sand." *New Yorker* 31 (April 16, 1955): 109–11.

Coke, Van Deren. *Taos and Santa Fe: The Artist's Environment, 1882–1942*. Albuquerque: University of New Mexico Press, 1963.

Cole, Mary. "Marsden Hartley's Poetry in Paint." *Art Digest* 25 (May 1, 1951): 17.

Davidson, Abraham. "Cubism and the Early American Modernist." *Art Journal* 26 (Winter 1966–67): 122–29.

Debrol, M. "Marsden Hartley—Painter of Mountains." *Creative Art* 2 (June 1928): xxxv–xxxvi.

Devree, Howard. "Expressionist Veins." *New York Times*, October 24, 1948, sec. 2, p. 9.

————. "A Reviewer's Notebook: In Galleries." *New York Times*, March 15, 1942, sec. 8, p. 5.

Dijkstra, Bram, ed. *A Recognizable Image: William Carlos Williams on Art and Artists*. New York: New Directions, 1978.

Eldredge, Charles. "Nature Symbolized: American Painting from Ryder to Hartley." In *The Spiritual in Art: Abstract Painting 1890–1985*, exhibition catalog. Los Angeles: Los Angeles County Museum of Art; New York: Abbeville Press, 1986, pp. 113–29. Discussion of Hartley's involvement with mysticism.

Feininger/Hartley, exhibition catalog. New York: Museum of Modern Art, 1944.

Gallup, Donald. "The Weaving of a Pattern: Marsden Hartley and Gertrude Stein." *Magazine of Art* 41 (November 1948): 256–61. On Hartley's friendship and correspondence with Gertrude Stein.

Greenberg, Clement. "Art." *Nation* 159 (December 30, 1944): 810; reprinted in *The Collected Essays and Criticism: Perceptions and Judgement, 1939–1944*, vol. 1, John O'Brian, ed., Chicago: University of Chicago Press, 1986, pp. 246–48.

Halasz, Piri. "Figuration in the '40s: The Other Expressionism." *Art in America* 70 (December 1982): 111–47.

Homer, William Innes. *Alfred Stieglitz and the American Avant-Garde*. Boston: New York Graphic Society. 1977.

Isaacson, Philip. "One Man's Treasure: An Art Critic Looks at the Hartley Memorabilia." *Bates College Alumni Magazine*, no. 3 (May 1984): 3–7.

Jaffe, Irma B. "Cubist Elements in the Painting of Marsden Hartley." *Art International* 14 (April 1970): 33–38.

Jewell, Edward Alden. "Art in Review: Pictures of New England by Marsden Hartley on View at the Downtown Gallery." *New York Times,* April 26, 1932, p. 24.

———. "What Is Imagination?—Doubts Surge Forward as Marsden Hartley Frames New Credo." *New York Times,* June 17, 1928, sec. 9, p. 19.

Kootz, Samuel. *Modern American Painters*. New York: Brewer and Warren, 1930.

Kramer, Hilton. "Hartley and Modern Painting." *Arts Magazine* 35 (February 1961): 42–45.

———. "Hartley's Lonely Vigil." *Art Digest* 28 (June 1954): 8, 23, 27.

Levin, Gail. "American Art." In *"Primitivism" in 20th Century Art*. Edited by

William Rubin. New York: Museum of Modern Art, 1985, pp. 452–73.

———. "Hidden Symbolism in Marsden Hartley's Military Pictures." *Arts Magazine* 54 (October 1979): 154–58.

———. "Marsden Hartley and the European Avant-Garde." *Arts Magazine* 54 (September 1979): 158–63.

———. "Marsden Hartley and Mysticism." *Arts Magazine* 60 (November 1985): 16–21.

———. "Marsden Hartley, Kandinsky, and Der Blaue Reiter." *Arts Magazine* 52 (November 1977): 156–60.

Ludington, Townsend. "The Quest for an American Style in the Paintings of Marsden Hartley." *National Humanities Newsletter* 8 (Fall 1986): 1–6.

McAlmon, Robert. *Distinguished Air (Grim Fairy Tales)*. Paris: Contact Editions, 1925. Hartley appears as one of the characters in this book situated in postwar Berlin.

McCausland, Elizabeth. "The Daniel Gallery and Modern American Art." *Magazine of Art* 44 (November 1951): 280–85.

———. "Hudson Walker's Recollections of the Artist in a Taped Interview." *Journal of the Archives of American Art* 8 (January 1968): 9–21.

———. "The Return of the Native." *Art in America* 40 (Spring 1952): 55–79.

———. "Tradition and Marsden Hartley." *Texas Quarterly* 5 (Winter 1962): 193–99.

Marling, William. "Marsden Hartley and William Carlos Williams: The Figure of a Friendship." *Arts Magazine* 55 (June 1981): 103–7.

Marsden Hartley/John Marin, exhibition catalog. Essays by Donald Brewer and Sheldon Reich. La Jolla, Calif.: La Jolla Museum of Art, 1964.

Mellquist, Jerome. *The Emergence of an American Art*. New York: Charles Scribner's Sons, 1942.

———. "Marsden Hartley." *Perspectives U.S.A.* 4 (Summer 1953): 62–77.

———. "Marsden Hartley, Visionary Painter." *Commonweal* 39 (December 31, 1943): 276–78.

Munson, Gorham. "The Painter from Maine." *Arts Magazine* 35 (February 1961): 33–41.

Nasgaard, Roald. *The Mystic North: Symbolist Landscape Painting in Northern Europe and North America 1890–1940*, exhibition catalog. Toronto: Art Gallery of Ontario and University of Toronto Press, 1984.

Needham, Gerald. "The Mystic North." *Art Journal* 44 (Summer 1984): 183–86.

Olds, David William. "A Study of Marsden Hartley's Mt. Katahdin Series, 1939–1942." Master's thesis, University of Texas, Austin, 1978.

Pardee, Hearne. "A Reading of Marsden Hartley." *Arts Magazine* 58 (September 1983): 104–6.

Pemberton, Murdock. "Soul Exposures." *Creative Art* 4 (January 1929): xlvii–xlix.

Perreault, John. "I'm Asking—Does It Exist? What Is It? Whom Is It For?" *Artforum* 19 (November 1980): 74–75. On art by gay artists.

Plagens, Peter. "Marsden Hartley Revisited or, Were We Really Ever There?" *Artforum* 7 (May 1969): 41–43.

Phillips, Duncan. "Marsden Hartley." *Magazine of Art* 37 (March 1944): 82–87.

Porter, Fairfield. "Reviews and Previews: Marsden Hartley." *Artnews* 56 (Summer 1957): 70.

Rexroth, Kenneth. *An Autobiographical Novel*. Garden City, N.Y.: Doubleday and Company, 1966.

Riley, Maude. "The Modern Shows Hartley and Feininger." *Art Digest* 19 (November 1, 1944): 6–7.

Rönnebeck, Arnold. "Hartley Gives Talk on 'The Original Research of Cezanne.'" *Rocky Mountain News* (Denver), March 25, 1928, p. 4.

Rose, Barbara. *American Painting: The Twentieth Century.* New York: Skira/Rizzoli, 1986.

Rosenfeld, Paul. "Marsden Hartley." In *Port of New York.* New York: Harcourt, Brace and Company, 1924; reprinted with an introduction by Sherman Paul, Urbana: University of Illinois Press, 1961.

———. "Marsden Hartley." In *Men Seen.* New York: Dial Press, 1925, pp. 177–88.

———. "Marsden Hartley." *Nation* 157 (September 18, 1943): 326–27. Obituary.

Schwartz, Sanford. "A Northern Seascape." *Art in America* 64 (January–February 1967): 72–76; reprinted in *The Art Presence,* New York: Horizon Press, 1982, pp. 53–63.

———. "When New York Went to New Mexico." *Art in America* 64 (July–August 1976): 93–97; reprinted in *The Art Presence,* pp. 85–94.

Scott, Gail R. "Marsden Hartley at Dog-town Common." *Arts Magazine* 54 (October 1979): 159–65.

———. "Metamorphosis of Idea: Marsden Hartley's Drawings." *Bates College Alumni Magazine,* no. 3 (May 1984): 8–13.

———. "The Surface of His Dignities." *Christian Science Monitor,* February 10, 1977, p. 28.

Seligmann, Herbert J. "The Elegance of Marsden Hartley—Craftsman." *International Studio* 74 (October 1921): l–liii.

———. "Marsden Hartley of Maine." *Down East* 3 (November–January 1956–57): 26–29, 40–41.

Stebbins, Theodore E., Jr., and Carol Troyen. *The Lane Collection: 20th-Century Paintings in the American Tradition,* exhibition catalog. Boston: Museum of Fine Arts, 1983.

Stein, Gertrude. *The Autobiography of Alice B. Toklas.* New York: Vintage Books, 1933, 1960.

Tashjian, Dickran. "Marsden Hartley and the Southwest: A Ceremony for Our Vision, A Fiction for the Eye." *Arts Magazine* 54 (April 1980): 127–31.

———. *Skyscraper Primitives: Dada and the American Avant-Garde, 1910–25.* Middletown, Conn.: Wesleyan University Press, 1975.

———. *William Carlos Williams and the American Scene,* exhibition catalog. Berkeley: University of California Press; New York: Whitney Museum of American Art, 1978.

Udall, Sharyn Rohlfsen. *Modernist Painting in New Mexico.* Albuquerque: University of New Mexico Press, 1984.

Walker, Hudson. "Marsden Hartley." *Kenyon Review* 9 (Spring 1947): 248–59.

Wells, Henry W. "The Pictures and Poems of Marsden Hartley." *Magazine of Art* 38 (January 1945): 26–30, 32.

Wertheim, Arthur Frank. *The New York Little Renaissance: Iconoclasm, Modernism and Nationalism in American Culture.* New York: New York University Press, 1976.

Williams, William Carlos. *The Autobiography of William Carlos Williams.* New York: New Directions, 1951.

———. "Beginnings: Marsden Hartley." *Black Mountain Review* 7 (Autumn 1957): 164–66; reprinted in *A Recognizable Image: William Carlos Williams on Art and Artists,* New York: New Directions, 1978, pp. 261–62.

Sources for Marginal Quotations

All quotations are by Marsden Hartley.

Page 9. Letter to Alfred Stieglitz, September 28, 1913, Hartley Archive, Yale Collection of American Literature, Beinecke Rare Book and Manuscript Library, Yale University (hereafter cited as *YCAL*).

Page 11. "Somehow a Past," 1933–c. 1939, unpublished manuscript, YCAL.

Page 21. Letter to Seumus O'Sheel, October 10, 1908, Hartley Archive, Archives of American Art, Smithsonian Institution, Washington, D.C. (hereafter cited as *AAA*).

Page 25. "291—and the Brass Bowl," 1934, in *America and Alfred Stieglitz: A Collective Portrait*, ed. Waldo Frank et al. (New York: Doubleday Doran & Co., 1934), pp. 236–42; reprinted in *On Art*, ed. Gail R. Scott (New York: Horizon Press, 1982), pp. 83, 84.

Page 26. "Somehow a Past," YCAL.

Page 34. "Whitman and Cézanne," in *Adventures in the Arts* (New York: Boni, Liveright, 1921; reprinted New York: Hacker Art Books, 1972), p. 33.

Page 44. Letter to Rockwell Kent, August 22, 1912, AAA.

Page 49. Statement for catalog of 1914 exhibition at 291; reprinted in *On Art*, p. 62.

Page 57. Statement for catalog of Forum Exhibition, 1916; reprinted in *On Art*, pp. 66–67.

Page 68. Letter to Alfred Stieglitz, October 9, 1919, YCAL.

Page 74. "Somehow a Past," YCAL.

Page 76. "The MOUNTAIN and the RECONSTRUCTION," 1928; reprinted in *On Art*, p. 76.

Page 81. Letter to Adelaide Kuntz, June 23, 1928, AAA.

Page 85. Letter to Adelaide Kuntz, September 22, 1929, AAA.

Page 90. "Somehow a Past," YCAL.

Page 94. "Soliloquy in Dogtown," c. 1931; reprinted in *The Collected Poems of Marsden Hartley*, ed. Gail R. Scott (Santa Rosa, Calif.: Black Sparrow Press, 1987), p. 175 (hereafter cited as *CP*).

Page 101. Letter to Adelaide Kuntz, January 18, 1934, AAA.

Page 111. Letter to Alfred Stieglitz, October 28, 1936, YCAL.

Page 113. "Fishermen's Last Supper," 1938; reprinted in *CP*, p. 271.

Page 117. "Is There an American Art,"

1938; reprinted in *On Art*, p. 199.

Page 123. "Pictures," 1941, in *Marsden Hartley/Stuart Davis* (Cincinnati: Modern Art Society, 1941); reprinted in *On Art*, p. 118.

Page 130. Letter to Adelaide Kuntz, October 24, 1939, AAA.

Page 137. "Story of a Defunct Mine," YCAL.

Page 141. "Reflex"; reprinted in *CP*, p. 210.

Page 142. "John Donne in His Shroud," c. 1940; reprinted in *CP*, p. 195.

Page 147. Letter to Alfred Stieglitz, June 1911, YCAL.

Page 151. "Is Art Necessary?" 1942, unpublished essay, YCAL.

Page 152. "On the Persistence of the Imagination," late 1930s; reprinted in *On Art*, p. 205.

Page 166. "On the Subject of Nativeness: A Tribute to Maine," 1937; reprinted in *On Art*, p. 114.

Page 167. "Georgia O'Keeffe: A Second Outline in Portraiture," 1936; reprinted in *On Art*, p. 106.

Page 168. Letter to Adelaide Kuntz, September 7, 1933.

Page 169. Letter to Adelaide Kuntz, November 6, 1935, AAA.

INDEX

Picture Credits

The photographers and the sources of photographic material other than those indicated in the captions are as follows:

Archives of American Art, Smithsonian Institution, Washington, D.C.: plates 2 (Alfred Valente Papers), 63, 144, 145, 152 (all Elizabeth McCausland Papers); Courtesy André Emmerich Gallery, New York: plates 36, 84; Adam Gordon, Philadelphia: plates 43, 81, 92; Marsden Hartley Memorial Collection, Museum of Art, Olin Arts Center, Bates College, Lewiston, Maine: plates 62, 127, 148, 151; Helga Photo Studio, Upper Montclair, New Jersey: plate 101; Courtesy Hirschl and Adler Galleries, Inc., New York: plates 57, 58, 61; P. M. Koch, Provincetown, Massachusetts: plate 118; Courtesy Gerald Peters Gallery, Santa Fe, New Mexico: frontispiece, plate 26; Adam Reich, New York: plate 135; George Roos, New York: plates 3, 68; Robert Rubic, New York: jacket front, plates 16, 29, 73, 76, 126; Courtesy Salander-O'Reilly Galleries, New York: plates 8, 10, 46, 74, 106, 122, 131; Sylvia Sarner, New York: plates 66, 124; Courtesy Gail R. Scott: plates 77, 120, 143, 146; Courtesy Leon Tebbetts: plate 150; Courtesy Vanderwoude Tananbaum Gallery, New York: plate 17.